Archaeological Survey of India

NOTES ON THE ANCIENT GEOGRAPHY OF GANDHARA

(A Commentary on a Chapter of Hiuan Tsang)

Archaeological Survey of India

NOTES ON THE ANCIENT GEOGRAPHY OF GANDHARA

(A Commentary on a Chapter of Hiuan Tsang)

A. FOUCHER

Translated by

H. HARGREAVES

GYAN

Published by

GYAN

Gyan Publishing House
5, Ansari Road
Daryaganj, New Delhi-110002
Phone: 011-47034999, 9811692060
E-mail: books@gyanbooks.com

Distribution Network
gyanbooks.com
India, USA, Canada, UK, Australia, France

ISBN : 978-81-212-2109-2 (HB)
First Published, 1915

2nd Impression 2021

Printed at: Gyan Press, Delhi.

Notes on the
Ancient Geography of Gandhara
Author: A. Foucher

Archæological Survey of India

NOTES

ON THE

ANCIENT GEOGRAPHY OF GANDHARA

(A Commentary on a Chapter of Hiuan Tsang)

BY

A. FOUCHER, Docteur es lettres.

TRANSLATED BY

H. HARGREAVES.

Superintendent, Hindu and Buddhist Monuments, Northern Circle.

CALCUTTA
SUPERINTENDENT GOVERNMENT PRINTING, INDIA
1915

TRANSLATOR'S PREFACE.

THE article by M. A. Foucher of which the following is a translation appeared under the title of *Notes sur la géographie ancienne du Gandhāra,* in the October issue of the *Bulletin de l'École française d'Extrême-Orient* in 1901. The article is not a new one, for twelve years have elapsed since its first publication, and it may be asked what can justify, after the lapse of such a period, the issue of an English translation. If any other justification than that of giving a new lease of life to an essay of such scientific value were necessary I would advance the plea that appearing in a publication not readily accessible to the Indian student and in a language less familiar than English its usefulness has been considerably circumscribed. Moreover, the recent excavations at Pushkarāvātī (Charsadda) by Sir John Marshall and Dr. J. Ph. Vogel and those of Dr. D. B. Spooner at the Kanishka *chaitya* (Shāh-jī-kī-ḍhērī) have directed renewed attention to this fascinating corner of India.

Wherever, since the first publication, exploration has been carried out on the sites indicated by M. Foucher footnotes will give the results and necessary references, results which cannot but increase the admiration of the reader for the learning and perspicacity displayed in the original essay.

The map and the majority of the text illustrations have been prepared for reproduction by Munshi Ghulam Muhammad and Babu Bhura Mal, draftsmen attached to the office of the Superintendent, Hindu and Buddhist Monuments, Northern Circle, Lahore, from materials kindly supplied by M. Foucher, while for the panoramic view of Shāhbāz-gaṛhi I am indebted to Khan Sahib Mian Wasi-ud-din of the Archæological Survey, Frontier Circle, Peshawar.

In conclusion, I would acknowledge the very valuable suggestions and encouragement received from Dr. J. Ph. Vogel and the liberality of the Government of the North-West Frontier Province which has rendered possible the publication of this volume.

H. HARGREAVES.

AUTHOR'S PREFACE.

IN the course of a scientific mission in India (1895—7) we visited in detail the Peshawar District which, as is well known, represents closely the territory of ancient Gandhāra. On this occasion we availed ourselves largely of the itinerary left by the Chinese pilgrim Hiuan-tsang, that "Pausanias of the Indianists" who made the same journey about twelve hundred and fifty years ago. In this region where there are scarcely any remains that are not Buddhist it indeed frequently happens that the predilections of the old pilgrim coincide with the present day interests of archæologists. We were, therefore, able to verify on the very spot, the accuracy of his account and to acquire some familiarity both with his methods of travel and the topography of the country. If it be allowed that the best way of identifying the itinerary of Hiuan-tsang in this country be to follow his wanderings it will then, we believe, be admitted that we are perhaps qualified to offer on this subject some notes which will at the same time throw some light upon the ancient geography of Gandhāra.

Now as we lay no claim to having made, properly speaking, any discovery, this enables us to discard from this article a number of profitless controversies which would have immoderately augmented it. There is not in reality a conceivable identification which has not been already advanced ; neither is there, except perhaps in the case of Peshawar, any which has not been contested, and is not, strictly speaking, capable of being called in question. For our part we leave Purushapura at Peshawar and Pushkarāvatī in the immediate neighbourhood of Charsadda but not so high as Mr. Garrick would have it nor so low as M. Vivien de Saint-Martin conjectured. We place also at the latter spot the famous "Stupa of the Eye Gift" which Cunningham, on the strength of a badly read passage in Song Yun, has somewhere located at Sahribahlol: neither is the identification of Shāhbāz-gaṛhi with Po-lu-sha anything new; it is one of two hypotheses which Cunningham has, successively, put forward for this spot. Even then it was so little proved, that in 1896, in a very interesting article Major, afterwards Colonel Sir Harold, Deane has been able to re-advance, without putting too much faith in it, the other hypothesis which puts Po-lu-sha at Paloḍhēri. Colonel Deane has also challenged the identification of Vivien de Saint-Martin which places U-to-kia-han-t' cha at Ohind or Und on the right bank of the Indus. But this is sufficient to show what a tissue of conjectures, often unjustifiable and sometimes even contradictory, the geography of Gandhāra is even yet. We will be content to bring forward in maps, sketches and plans the reasons determining our opinion and to point out by notes where it agrees or differs from those already expressed. Competent persons will be able to distinguish, without it being necessary to lose one's time in idle discussions, the degree of coherence and precision which we shall be able to bring to bear on these questions in default of that certainty which only authentic inscriptions found *in situ* can really give.

The exceptional interest both from the historical and archæological point of view presented by the high road of all the old conquerors of India and by the inexhaustible mine of the best Græco-Buddhist sculptures known, would be, if such were necessary, our excuse for returning again to and treating at such length, the ancient geography of the country of Gandhāra.

We are especially indebted to M. H. Parmentier, architect and member of l'École française d'Extrême-Orient who has been good enough to prepare from our photographs the numerous sketches which so excellently illustrate this article.

A. FOUCHER.

LIST OF ILLUSTRATIONS.

ANCIENT GEOGRAPHY OF GANDHĀRA.

WE join Hiuan-tsang at the moment when coming from the west, he reaches Gandhāra, after crossing mountains and valleys, by the old road, still marked by *stupas*, through the Khyber Pass. We can imagine him ambling along, on his mule, like the Chinese traveller shown on a jade sculpture[1] in the Lahore Museum, (Fig. 1) or as one still sees the pilgrims from Central Asia passing along to embark at some Indian port for Mecca.

Fig. 1. Chinese Traveller.

Although he begins by giving this kingdom—at that time without a king—a much more considerable area, the account of his travels refers exclusively to that plain which forms at the present time the district of Peshawar and which is, in fact, entirely hemmed in within its girdle of mountains linked by the River Indus.[2] Not only depopulated but more than half ruined by the evils of war did he find this

---

1 This little bas-relief is carved on a piece of rough jade measuring about 0·20 m. in length. Like most of the objects preserved in the Lahore Museum its origin is very uncertain. All that can be asserted of it is that it is exhibited in a case reserved specially for a number of specimens of Græco-Buddhist art coming from Rokhri on the Indus and which an inundation of the river brought to light. The choice of material and the style of the subject betray very clearly its Chinese origin and if, indeed, found in the sands of the Indus it must be admitted that it was brought into Northern India by way of an *ex voto* by one of the many Chinese Buddhist pilgrims. It seems in every way more consistent with reality than the pictures which show Hiuan-tsang on foot bowed beneath the burden of his baggage the disagreement of which with the texts Mr. Bharth has pointed out (*Le Pelerin I-tsing, Journal des Savants*, 1898, 2nd article, p. 28, of the reprint : for the pictures of Hiuan-tsang see *The Japanese Pantheon*, by Hoffmaun in Von Siebold's *Nippon*, Vol. V, and the Japanese review *Hansei Zasshi*, Vol. XXII, No. II, p. 25).

[This jade sculpture is no longer traceable in the Lahore Museum. *Trans.*]

2 See the map attached to this article. Hiuan-tsang says " 1000 *li* from east to west and 800 *li* from north to south," in round numbers say 300 kilometres and 250 kilometres and, on the other hand a dozen marches or so were sufficient to allow him to visit the country, the boundaries of which to the east and north by the Indus which separated it from the kingdom of Takshaśila and by the mountains of Swāt and Bunēr which separated it from Udyāna, he moreover describes perfectly. It must then be admitted, either, as is usually conceded, that Gandhāra extended far beyond the natural boundaries to the south and west, or else that Hiuan-tsang's figures, elsewhere fairly accurate, give us double the real extent in both directions. We should be disposed to adopt the latter view. It is very easy indeed to push back the western frontier of Gandhāra as far as Kunar and Jallalahād in order to locate it 1000 *li* to the west of the Indus as do Vivien de Saint-Martin (*Mémoire analytique* p. 307) and Cunningham (*Ancient Geography of India*, p. 48) but how then are to be found between Kunar and the Hindu Kush " the 600 *li* from west to east " of the kingdom of Nagarhāra and, " the 1000 *li* circumference " of that of Lampāka not to

country which had always so much to endure from being on the high road of all the conquerors of India. But the worst invasions were yet to come and Gandhāra at least remained Indian in manners and language; it is well known that this is no longer the case.[1] It is not here as in Kashmir where the mass of the people have not changed, and even after having become for the greater part Mahommedan have preserved with their language, the ancient names of places and the old legends. The Afghans of the Yusufzai clan are as little familiar as anyone with the antiquities of a country, which they have occupied for only five centuries and where their first care was to drive out or exterminate as completely as possible the few inhabitants.[2] In our days when under the rule of the Sikhs and their successors the English, Gandhāra again became part of India, it was all too late to revive the past. In the presence of the inscriptions of Aśoka, cows are slaughtered and it is "Pushtu" that is spoken in the birth-place of Panini! It is true, there seems to remain a residue of the Hindu population, *banya* families, scattered here and there, in the larger villages and whom for the sake of their trade, the Pathans, unable to keep accounts and in consequence incapable of shop-keeping, have always been obliged to tolerate. But with some rare exceptions it does not appear to us that these Hindus have preserved, through such a long period of subjection, any remembrance from the time of their independence.[3] We do not believe that there will be

---

mention Kapiśa? Let us mention also that if the distances assigned by Hiuan-tsang in the general direction of east and west between the Hindu-Kush and the Indus be added together, *viz.*, 600 *li* from Kapiśa to Lampāka, 300 *li* for Lampāka (he gives 1000 *li* in circuit), 100 *li* from Lampāka to Nagarahāra, 600 *li* for Nagarahāra, 500 *li* from Nagarahāra to Gandhāra, 1000 *li* for Gandhāra, a total of 3100 *li* or nearly 1000 kilometres is obtained. Now the distance as the crow flies is only 300 kilometres to which it is sufficient to add, as is generally done, one-third more to allow for the irregularities of the surface and the windings of the road. Should we extend the road to 500 kilometres it would still be less than half Hiuan-tsang's data. How then is this serious and persistent error in sum to be reconciled with the perfect and constant accuracy of the details? Did he learn by hearsay the extent of the kingdoms and hand them down upon trust without dreaming of checking them by his own observations? Or rather may it not be that when editing the *Si-yu-ki* he is himself deceived when estimating them by badly interpreting the accurate data of his own itinerary? It seems, in fact, as if he calculates the extent of the different countries, not from frontier to frontier but from each capital to the two neighbouring capitals on his line of march and so in this way adds the same number twice. It is, therefore, allowable to ask one's self if he did not arrive at this figure of 1000 *li* for the extent of Gandhāra from east to west by adding to the distance from Purushapura to Nagarahāra (500 *li*) that which in its turn separated Purushapura from the capital of the neighbouring kingdom to the east, namely Takshaśila (9 stages, *i.e.*, 450 or 500 *li*). In the same way the 600 *li* from east to west of the kingdom of Nagarahāra seems to be made up of these 500 *li* between Nagarahāra and Purushapura to the east *plus* the 100 *li* mentioned elsewhere between Nagarahāra and Lampāka to the west: and so on, the identity of the name of the capital and the kingdom moreover aiding the confusion.

[1] It appears that this was the case as early as the beginning of the XVIth Century. "After having crossed the Sind (Indus)," Baber tells us, "the soil, water, trees, stones, people, costumes and customs all appertain to Hindustan" (*Memoirs* translated by Pavet de Courteille II, p. 182). For Hiuan-tsang on the contrary India commenced almost at the foot of the Hindu-Kush after leaving Kapiśa.

[2] Concerning the Afghans, or, as they call themselves Pathāns and their invasions see the *Lettres sur l'Inde* and the introduction to the *Chants populaires des Afghans* by J. Darmesteter. On the present distribution of the clans see our account of a journey *Sur la frontière indo-afghane*, p. 179: the reader will forgive us for having to refer so often to the last named work for all additional details which would uselessly encumber this article.

[3] More than eight centuries after the Mussalman conquest the Sikhs found many Hindus settled at Peshawar. General Court says, "The population of Peshawar may be rated at 80,000 souls, consisting of Afghans, Kashmirians and Indians. The latter appear to have been its primitive inhabitants, but although they are still very numerous, they live in dependence on the Mahomedans and are still oppressed by heavy taxation. All the commerce of the country is in their hands" (*J. A. S. B.*, 1836, p. 476). We have gathered the same impression. In all the villages of any importance not only in the Peshawar District where under British rule security has become greater, but in the independent territory of Yāghistan, beyond the administrative frontier, as for example in Swāt, there are little bazars occupied by Hindu merchants who, though greatly despised and not always paid, do not complain very much of their lot and above all, according to them do not remember that their family had ever lived anywhere else (cf. *Sur la frontière, indo-afghane*, p. 106, 148, etc.). Dr. Stein has since made the same declaration regarding Bunēr and also considers that these *banyas* "represent the trading castes of the old Hindu population which had remained in these valleys after the Pathan invasion" (*Detailed Report of an Archæological Tour with the Buner Field Force*, Lahore 1898, p. 24. Republished in the *Ind. Antiq.* 1899, p. 24).

any more to expect, as regards historical traditions, from the tribe of the Gujars, herdsmen who are nomadic and, besides, converted to Islam and whose whole existence is absorbed in the carc of their buffaloes—nor from those unhappy "heathen" of Kafiristan who appear to be the authentic descendants of the original inhabitants and whom the Afghans of the Amir continue to hunt out even in their last mountain refuge. It is not, therefore, to be wondered at, if wanting local traditions, we are obliged to seek in the "Memoirs" of foreign pilgrims information regarding the period anterior to the Mahommedan invasions, at a time when Indian life had not entirely disappeared from Gandhāra. It will also be understood why in this country, though doubly classical, where (the stones at every step still prove it) Indian thought was once wedded to the forms of Greek art, we find so often the old names of localities replaced by new and barbarous denominations. It will, therefore, be conceded that in order to establish our identifications, we should have recourse not to etymology, which here more than elsewhere is liable to be deceptive, but to topographical and archæological arguments and, above all, to the material evidence of the ruins: here the past has nothing left but these dumb witnesses.

Not only does the Sunni fanaticism of the Yusufzai Afghans seem to have made every effort to efface all remembrance of the times of the "Kafirs" but their characteristic Mussalman indolence has succeeded in changing even the face of the country. True, it is still "rich in cereals," at least where the canals of the Indian period, which the Pathans had allowed to fall into disuse, have been reopened by the English engineers. It has even been possible recently to recommence the cultivation of the sugar-cane which Hiuan-tsang mentions and which had been almost entirely abandoned, and the well watered gardens of Peshawar and Mardan still "produce a variety of flowers and fruits." But though the climate is still so favoured that snow is almost unknown in the plain it has now none of that humidity so extolled in days of yore.[1] The water (and this is a point to keep in mind) has almost everywhere disappeared from the slopes of the denuded hills where the ruins often extensive, testify that it once flowed close to the convents which, without it, could not have existed and would not even have been built. The present villagers claim to recollect a time when the springs still gushed forth in the hollows of ravines which to-day are dry. If they are asked what has become of them, they invariably reply that the wicked "heathen" before abandoning the country to the Moslims carefully closed them up. The strange part is that they are not always wrong, for in fact in the Adinzai valley in Swāt, at the foot of the Laram Hills, has been found a spring which had been hermetically closed by means of a little *stūpa* dome.[2] But it is obvious that the malice of the "Kafirs" is not a sufficient reason to account for so general a desiccation of which we have heard people complain even in

---

[1] Song-yun draws us a most pleasing picture of the environs—now so very barren—of Shāhbāz-gaṛhi (Beal, *Buddhist Records* I, p. XCVII and CII). "There is nothing so beautiful as the gardens of Peshawar in the spring," says Baber (*loc. land.* II p. 77) and elsewhere he tells us of thick jungles between Makām and the Indus (*ibid*, p. 52) or round about Peshawar (*ibid*, p. 135) where he hunted the rhinoceros and also the tiger near Nowshera (*ibid*, p. 77). Even to-day the crest of the hill of Karamār is covered with magnificent trees which owe their preservation entirely to the sanctity of the neighbouring *ziārat*. Trees are being again planted along the roads across these shadeless plains but the perfectly classical nudity of its mountains remains one of the most striking features of the landscape of Gandhāra.

[2] See Colonel Deane, *Note on Udyāna and Gandhāra* (*J. R. A. S.* 1896, p. 659. Cf. *Sur la frontière indo-afghane*, p. 68). Concerning this question of the increasing scarcity of water in the district see the *Report on Yūsufzzis* by Dr. Bellew, p. 22.

Kashmir. Are we then to believe in a vast change of climatic conditions which would moreover have extended to all Central Asia? If one reflects that the Mussalmans, who are burners of wood, have everywhere, save around their *ziārats*, destroyed the trees once venerated by the Hindus who are burners of cow-dung, it seems that the most simple and obvious explanation of the present aridity is to be found in the thoughtless disafforestation of the country.

May we be allowed one last observation apropos of this preface of Hiuan-tsang? In round figures he estimates the number of convents in Gandhāra at about a thousand and although in his time the greater part were already deserted and in ruins, one would still be able easily to make out the traces of more than a hundred. Now in the pages which follow Hiuan-tsang tells us of barely fifteen preferably chosen among the few which were still inhabited. Let us not forget, in short, that he is a pilgrim and not an archæologist. He is more concerned with the religious merit than with the artistic interest of the monuments and prefers the society of a living monk to the sight of the most beautiful ruins. If we consider this, it will perhaps astonish us less that he could not have foreseen the fame which the two sites now known as Jamāl-Gaṛhī and Takht-i-Bāhī would come to enjoy among European scholars.

Let us even confess that it would be somewhat naive to imagine that among the number, he should have mentioned and described precisely those two for the simple reason that the excavations carried out there in our days have made them more familiar to us than any others.

I.—Purushapura.

We have now reached *Po-lu-sha-pu-lo*, that is to say *Purushapura*. That this town is the *Purushavar* or *Purshavar* of Al-biruni, the *Pershavar* or *Peishavar* of Abul Fazl and the Peshawar of the present day, nobody denies; for once, on one point, all are agreed.[1] Hiuan-tsang estimates the circumference of the city, only one corner of which was still occupied by a thousand families, as about 40 *li* or 12 kilometres. This is about one third more than the present circumference of the mud walls of Peshawar—at least of the native "City" (as distinct from the European cantonment) which, in all probability, still occupies the site of the old town.[2] Now in the city or its immediate neighbourhood, Hiuan-tsang makes mention of two important religious foundations, and it is worth while endeavouring if we can still find any traces of them in the direction he indicates and preferably, according to the observation justly made by Colonel Deane, in some place still reverenced by the *banyas* of the bazar. If the Hindu community has been anywhere strong enough to preserve a tradition, surely it will be in the capital city. But we must bear in mind that all old Indian shrines were not, on that account necessarily Buddhist. Hiuan-tsang admits the existence of a hundred Brahmanical temples in the country though in the sequel he mentions in particular, only two.

[1] The credit of this identification which has had the rare good fortune of being universally accepted dates back it seems to H. Wilson (*J. R. A. S.*, Vol. 5, 1839, p. 118). Before him Abel-Remusat had believed he identified in the Fo-lu-sha of Fa-hien "the Beluchis."

[2] At least we have no reason to suppose the contrary. Colonel Deane who has first advanced the hypothesis of a displacement of the city has nothing to mention in support of this opinion except a recent and trifling encroachment of the 'Commissariat Lines' on the west side (*J. R. A. S.*, p. 666). We have not, however, on the indications of our pilgrims, anything to look for in that direction.

"Inside the royal city, towards the north-east, is an old foundation (or a ruinous foundation). Formerly this was the precious tower of the *pātra* (begging bowl) of Buddha."[1] Two centuries before, Fa-Hian had found this *stūpa* served by nearly seven hundred monks who inhabited a neighbouring *saṅghārāma* or monastery. Twice a day, a little before noon and in the evening, they offered the precious relic for the worship of the faithful who strove emulously to fill it with offerings. But at the time of Hiuan-tsang's visit the bowl after many vicissitudes, had gone to Persia and the sanctuary was ruined and deserted. Now at the north-east of the native city between the Grand Trunk Road and the modern railway there still exists a large Hindu establishment, known by the name of *Pañj-tirath*, in Sanskrit *Pañcha tirtha*. It contains actually, as the name indicates, five little tanks which are the *tirthas* or holy bathing places shaded by some sacred fig trees (*aśvattha* or *pipal*) and surrounded by some miserable modern buildings; but it cannot be doubted that the site is ancient and the *purohitas* or officiating Brahmans of the place do not hesitate to trace the origin, as is the custom in Northern India for all the sanctuaries of which the true legend is lost, back to the five sons of Pāṇḍu, the heroes of the *Mahābhārata*. Unfortunately the place has been too much disturbed and the indications of the pilgrims are too vague to allow us to affirm anything in a decisive fashion : at all events we are convinced that it is somewhere near the *Pañj-tirath* that following right methods, first of all search should be made for the site of the *Pātra-chaitya*.

Fig. 2. The Buddha's Alms Bowl.

Hiuan-tsang continues "outside the city, about 8 or 9 *li* to the south-east, there is a *pipal* tree about 100 feet or so in height." Tao-yong tells us also of this tree which is, in reality, as he says, the kind of fig tree under which the Buddha attained enlightenment. In his time the planting of it was attributed to King Kanishka. A century later Hiuan-tsang was assured quite seriously that the four past Buddhas had sat in its shade which would give it an age of several *kalpas* and consequently, make it survive the periodic dissolutions of the world! It is singular that nine hundred years afterwards one of the first visits of Baber to Bēgrām as he called Peshawar, had for its object a tree of colossal proportions. To-day we have only to choose and we could easily recognize it, or at least some offshoot of it, in the direction indicated by the pilgrims : but there has already been too much archæological romancing with regard to India for us to try our hand at it.[2]

[1] Stanislas Julien's slip of north-west for north-east has been corrected by Beal (*Buddhist Records* I.—p. 98 n. 58) : for the references of Fa-hien see Beal (*ibid*, p. XXXIII) and Legge's translation p. 35. No identification has been suggested for the *Pātra-chaitya*. Colonel Deane certainly mentions the Pañj-tirath in his article (*loc. laud.*, p. 666), but makes no use of it—we give (fig. 2) an illustration of the Buddha's alms bowl from a relief preserved in the Lahore Museum; it is exhibited as a relic on a throne under a canopy.

[2] See Tao-yong, translation Beal (*loc. laud.*, Vol. I. p. cv); Bāber (*Memoires*, Pavet de Courteille, p. 322) or Erskine (translation, p. 157). Cunningham is of opinion that it may be still the same tree (*Arch. Survey of India*, Vol. II, p. 88). Sacred fig-trees are, however, too common in the neighbourhood of Peshawar for it to be necessary to look for that of Kanishka, as Colonel Deane does, in the Pipal Mandi, inside the city and in the opposite direction to that indicated by the Chinese pilgrims (*loc. laud.*, p. 666 —Cf. *Sur la frontière indo-afghane*, p. 212).

Indeed we should not even have spoken of it, had Hiuan-tsang not mentioned in its immediate neighbourhood and to the south (Tao-yong says expressly that the tree was situated "a hundred paces to the north-west of the pagoda") the famous religious foundation of King Kanishka. All the Chinese pilgrims who have left us accounts of their travels in northern India describe it in the same way. Fa-Hian is the first to tell us the legend of its miraculous origin which Song-yun repeats and which Hiuan-tsang takes up in his turn.

Ou-k'ong mentions it first among the three which he ascribes to King Kanishka. Al-biruni in the 11th century still knows "the vihara of Purushavar" by the name of "Kanik-chaitya."[1] The witnesses of its splendour and even of its decay are never tired of dwelling upon the height of the *stūpa*, the loftiest in India, nor upon the monumental proportions of the monastery which adjoined on the west side. Nor are they less in agreement on the site of these two edifices. Tao-yong who probably took the southern extremity of the city as his starting point places them four *li* or a little less than a kilometre to the east, Song-yun setting out further north puts them 7 *li* or two kilometres to the south-east. Hiuan-tsang finally states, as we have seen, 8 or 9 *li* or nearly three kilometres to the south-east;[2] but he reckons from the *Pātra-chaitya*, that is to say, from the north-east corner of the royal city, so that in reality their evidence agrees and if we follow their guidance, we cannot but seek for the foundation of the great Indo-Scythian king on the south-east outskirts of Peshawar.

Now, if we set out by the Lahore gate and take the Cherat Road or that of Hazar Khāni we shall meet about a kilometre to the south-east of the present walls of the city a group of dusty mounds which, although in a lamentable condition, yet mark an important site.[3] Composed of stones, burnt bricks and fine grey earth, which seems to be the remains of ancient unburnt bricks, they have been for centuries subjected to regular exploitation by the builders from the neighbouring great city and by the cultivators of the vicinity. It is well known that freestone is as rare as sought after on these alluvial plains where it has to be brought

---

[1] See Fa-hien translation, Beal, p. XXXII and Legge translation, page 33; Song-yun and Tao-yong, Beal translation, p. CIII; *l'Itinéraire d'Ou-K'ong*, by M. M. Chavannes and S. Levi (*J. A.* 1895, p. 357); Alberuni, *India*; Sachau, translation Vol. II, p. 11. Five centuries later the only celebrated holy place at Bēgram which Bāber speaks of in his *Memoires* is the Gor Khattri (Cf. translation, Pavet de Courteille who writes Gouri-Ketri and Kourh-Ketri, Vol. I, p. 322 and Vol. II, p. 78, and Erskine, translation, who writes Gūrh Katri, p. 157 and 264). It required nothing more to suggest to Cunningham the identification of the Gor Khattri site, where stands Akbar's caravanserai—now the local administration offices—with that of Kanishka's convent (*A. S. R.*, Vol. II, p. 89 and *Ancient Geography of India*, p. 81) and M. J. Darmesteter echoes this theory (*Lettres sur l' Inde*, p. 26. Cf. *Sur la frontière indo-afghane*, p. 214 and fig. 39). Now if we return to the detailed account given by Bāber we read :—

1. That the Gor Khattri was "one of the holy places of the Yogis of the Hindus who come from great distances to cut off their hair and shave their beards," in other words it was a place of pilgrimage where the laity came to perform the *śraddha* or funeral sacrifices in honour of their ancestors and which religious mendicants frequented in great numbers as is still the case at Hardwār, Thānesar, etc.
2. That the monument consisted of cells and underground galleries where access was only possible by crawling, and where in these little cells lived numerous *yogīs* and sādhus—in short, it was something resembling the subterranean temples that are still to be seen at Prayāg (Allahabād), Ujjain, etc. Of the thoroughly Brahmanical character of the shrine there is no doubt and there is no basis for its identification with Kanishka's monastery. The ground cleared of this useless hypothesis, it appears to us to be preferable to follow in all simplicity the topographical indications given by the Chinese pilgrims.

[2] The mistake of Hiuan-tsang's biographer who writes "80 or 90 *li*" instead of 8 or 9 *li* has been already corrected by Vivien de Saint Martin (*loc. laud.*, p. 308).

[3] See the map of the environs of Peshawar which we reproduce from that of an inch to the mile published by the Survey of India, Calcutta. At the same time we give a plan and a sketch of Shāh-jī-ki-ḍhērī (Fig. 3).

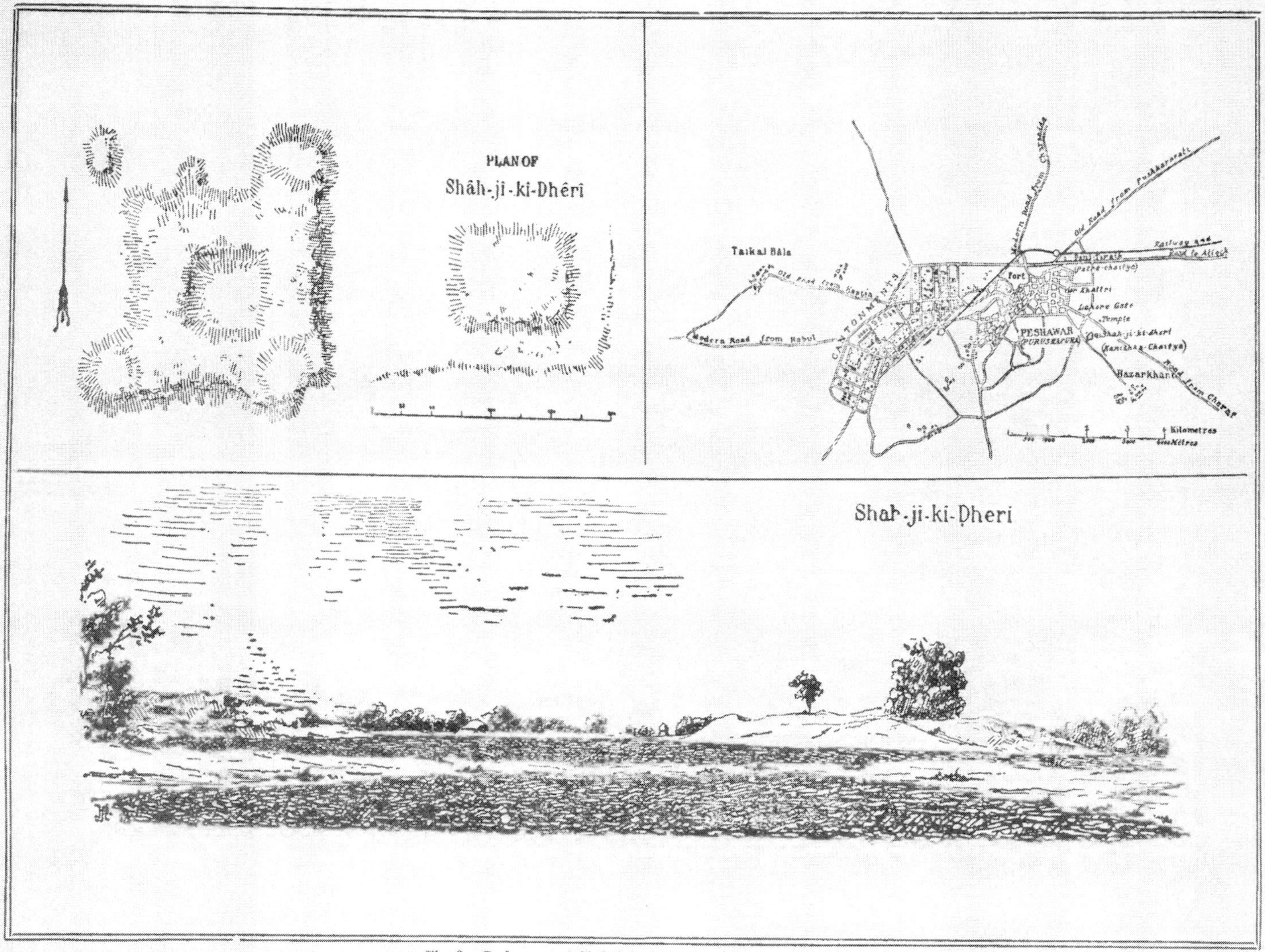

Fig. 3. Peshawar and Shâh-ji-ki-ḍhêrī, (Kanishka-chaitya).

at great expense from the nearest mountains; the large ancient bricks, which cost only the trouble of collecting, sell for more in the bazar than new ones and the very earth so fine and powdery forms an excellent manure for the crops. Thus whilst the building materials hidden under these mounds take the road to the city, their very dust is scattered over the adjoining fields. It is astonishing that at the p esent time anything of them should still exist.

Such, however, was their extent in days gone by that some hillocks, their sides riven by excavations and hollowed by the rains, still successfully resist the attacks of cultivation. For many years they will continue to preserve from oblivion their stately, and perhaps historic, name of *Shāh-jī-kī-ḍheri*, in Sanskrit *Mahārāja chaitya*, in English "the mound of the great king."[1] Moreover, one cannot help noticing that of the two chief mounds the more easterly one has precisely the three hundred metres or thereabouts in circumference which the Chinese pilgrims give as an average to the "pagoda" of King Kanishka. Song-yun and Too-yong, who found it still in existence state respectively 300 and 390 paces; Hiuan-tsang says one *li* and a half, but he saw it only in ruins. The elongated shape of the tumulus is easily explained by the fact that on the east side a flight of steps, as we know from the same source, led to the top of the *stūpa*. If finally one is surprised to find nothing more than a mound rising some four or five metres at the site of "the highest pagoda in Jambudvipa" one has only to remember that the upper stories were of wood and it had been several times destroyed by fire. Song-yun tells us that it had been three times burnt down by fire from heaven and three times restored. At the time of Hiuan-tsang's visit it had again been reduced to ashes for the fourth time: "steps are being taken for its restoration, but they are not yet complete." Both the pious travellers relate the same legend according to which after the seventh time the law of the Buddha would become finally extinct in the country. But we know not if the prophecy was fulfilled

Fig. 4. Kanishka-chaitya after excavation.

[1] Colonel Deane in his article mentions these tumuli but does not think of turning them to account (*loc. laud.*, p. 666). Care must be taken not to confuse them with any of those mounds, so numerous in the outskirts of Peshawar, which have been formed by the accumulation of rubbish from brick kilns.

and whether the *stūpa* was burnt down seven times before the arrival of the Mahommedans.[1]

More characteristic still is the other *ḍhērī* situated to the west and quite near to the former at the very spot where Hiuan-tsang places the monastery connected with the *stūpa*. It is almost square in form with sides measuring not less than 200 metres. In the middle there is a pronounced rectangular depression, whilst the raised edges immediately suggest the idea of four blocks of buildings enclosing an inner courtyard according to the usual plan of both ancient *saṅghārāmas* and modern *serais*. The vast proportions of the quadrangle and its strongly bastioned corners, (that of the north-west has indeed been separated from the mass but not levelled by the destroyers) recall especially Hiuan-tsang's account of the importance of the convent, of its double storied pavilions and its high corner-towers. In his time it was "somewhat decayed." Since that time fire has destroyed the verandahs and "belvederes" and the other wooden structures. In the complete collapse the inner and even the outer walls, constructed of unburnt brick or merely beaten clay, as is still the custom of the country, have crumbled away through the action of the sun and the rain, covering the stone and brick substructions. In this way are formed here, as in many other places, these ash-coloured mounds which still vaguely outline on the plain in faint ruined relief, the form of the buildings of old.

That both the convent and the neighbouring *stūpa*, had been the prey of the flames is not a mere conjecture. On several occasions these ruins have been the object of excavations, carried out *manu militari* by parties of sepoys. Side by side with the haphazard excavations of the collectors of building materials and manure can be distinguished some systematically bored tunnels which disclose the foundations and the sides of which are speckled by the charcoal of the old conflagrations. We have no hesitation in saying that these excavations could have been better conducted. Instead of attacking directly the mass of *débris*, it would have been, we believe, more advantageous both with a view to the identification of the site and of possible finds to explore the immediate surroundings. It would have been particularly interesting to ascertain if the remains of "the hundred little *stūpas*" which Hiuan-tsang mentions on the right and left of the great pagoda, still exist.[2] Besides the fact that they have had more chances of escape, if not from the depredations of treasure hunters at least from the ravages of fire, we are told that the workmen had lavished on them all their skill. Just on these sides are some earthworks of ancient origin, which already the crops are invading but where the fragments of brick are so compact in places as to resist the primitive plough of the country. Whatever may have been the manner in which the excavations have been conducted, they have at least resulted in establishing the Buddhist and even the so-called Græco-Buddhist character of the ruins. They have, in fact, brought to light some statues, which leave no doubt on this point whilst some vases full of flour found in the large *ḍhērī* on the west finally confirm the hypothesis of a convent.[3]

---

[1] Song-yun tells us expressly that, "the roof consisted of every kind of wood" (Beal, p. CIV.) Cf. what Hiuan-tsang tells us later in connection with the wood used in the construction of the '*stūpa* of the Eye-Gift' at Pushkarāvatī.

[2] That is to the north and to the south, the *stūpa* being orientated towards the east by its flight of steps.

[3] Besides the idle talk of the villagers concerning discoveries of *buts* that is idols, and vessels full of flour or even in the popular imagination of gold, we possess on this point the well founded evidence of Colonel Deane (*loc. laud.*, p. 666).

To the chain of our presumptions one last link is still wanting. It is indeed the rule in Mussalman India that the ancient Hindu sites were very soon adapted to the new religion by some sacred tomb or even a mosque. This law which in Kashmir is universal we see repeatedly verified in Gandhāra despite the most unfavourable circumstances. Here also, on the south of the big mound, many Mahommedan tombs are crowded together under some trees round the *ziārat* of Roshyān Shāh. But of the ancient sanctity of the spot we possess another testimony infinitely more to the point. At some distance to the north at the same place where we should expect to find the fig tree of Kanishka there stands a little octagonal shrine of Mughal architecture which is in reality a Hindu temple. The passing *sādhus* and *yōgīs* often find shelter here. Every year the Hindus of the neighbourhood resort to the spot for a *mēla*, partly fair, partly pilgrimage, as our "*pardons*" of Brittany. "When is this *mēla* held?"—"In the month of Hār." Now Hār is the Hindi *Āsāhr* and the Sanskrit *Āshāḍha* which corresponds to June-July and the festival of *Āshāḍha* was the anniversary of the conception of the Buddha on the occasion of his last appearance on this earth.

We do not wish to urge any further the identification of a site which we have not excavated. We will only say in summing up the results of our observations and enquiries that at the place indicated by the Chinese pilgrims, on a site still worshipped by the Hindus on a date which is traditionally Buddhist and the name of which preserves the memory of a royal foundation, we find the ruins of two edifices proved by excavation to be Buddhist and which by their dimensions and relative position, correspond in a singular way, even after the changes wrought by men and time, to the description handed down by eye witnesses of the *stūpa* and monastery attributed to King Kanishka. Before trying to find the position of these two monuments elsewhere it will, first of all, have to be demonstrated that all these concordances are delusive.[1]

II.—Pushkarāvatī.

From Purushapura Hiuan-tsang takes us to Pushkarāvatī. In proceeding there, he only continues to follow the high road of India. The route of those days avoided, and for very good reasons, entering upon the swamps and next the stony deserts furrowed by torrents, which regardless of expense, the modern road from Peshawar to Attock now crosses. Instead of taking a short cut, it wound leisurely in a north-easterly direction towards the most level, most fertile and most populous parts of Gandhāra. Just as to-day it leads in one stage to the first of the "Eight-

[1] The correctness of M. Foucher's identification was fully proved by Dr. D. B. Spooner whose exploration of the Shāh-jī-kī-ḍhērī site in 1908-09 laid bare the remains of the main *stūpa* and recovered the inscribed relic casket with crystal reliquary from the centre of the monument. The most interesting of the four epigraphs on the casket has been translated by the learned discoverer as "The slave (or servant) Agisala, the overseer of works at Kanishka's *vihara* in the *saṅghārāma* of Mahāsēna." The *ka* of *Kanashkasa* is the least certain of the *aksharas* but the figure of the king himself, exactly as depicted on his coins, represented standing between two attendants on the main portion of the casket, leaves no doubt on the point, while the only coin found by the side of the deposit was one of that monarch. The relics were presented by the Government of India to the Burmese Buddhists to be re-enshrined at Mandalay; the casket is still preserved in the Peshawar Museum (cf. *Excavations at Shāh-jī-kī-ḍhērī, A. S. I., 1908-09, pp. 38ff*).

Dr. Spooner's excavation of the western mound amply proved its Buddhist character and the further examination by Mr. H. Hargreaves in 1910-11 confirmed this, disclosing remains of massive brick columns and enormous walls pointing not only to the former existence of imposing structures but also to a prolonged occupation of the site (cf. *Excavations at Shāh-jī-kī-ḍhērī, A. S. I. 1910-11, pp. 25ff* [*Translator*]).

towns " (Hashtnagar), so did it then to the flourishing city of Pushkarāvatī. Situated on the left bank " of a large river " this town with its circumference of four or five kilometres (fourteen or fifteen *li*) must have covered the entire site at present

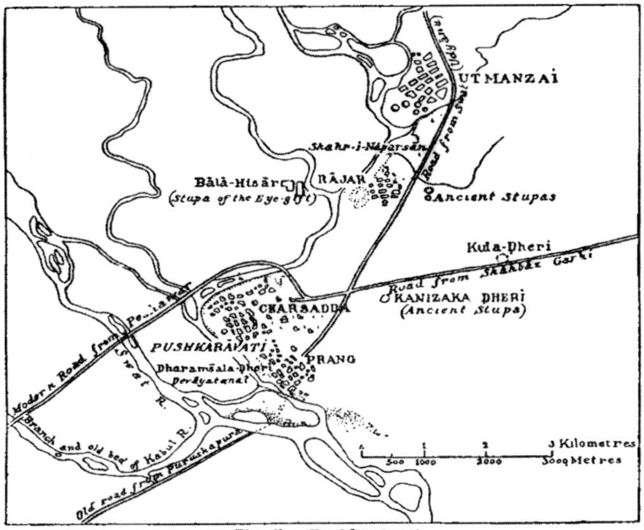

Fig. 5. Pushkarāvati.

occupied by the large villages of Prāng and Charsadda,[1] including their cemeteries : for the dead take up no less room than the living. We are led to think that the junction of the *Kubhā* and *Suvastu*, to-day very much lower down stream, once took place at this point, not only from the evidence of the Chinese travellers who speak of only one river to cross, but also from the name of " Prāng " which has no meaning in Pushtu and which we have already met with in Kashmir in the sense of Prayāg, that is to say confluence.[2] The change in their point of junction would be only one of a hundred examples of the changeable mood of Indian rivers. Moreover, one of the branches of the Kābul River continues to empty itself into the Swāt immediately below Prāng. Let us add in passing that for the people of the country the latter still remains the " big stream " of which the other is only a tributary.

However probable the identification of Pushkarāvatī as suggested by Cunningham long ago may be, yet it requires to be confirmed in detail by that of the monuments which Hiuan-tsang enumerates in the neighbourhood of the town. These are :—

1. At the west a Brahmanical temple.
2. On the east a *stūpa* built by Aśoka.
3. On the north another *stūpa* very high and flanked by its monastery.

Can we not find some traces, at least, of these buildings? The hypothesis will hold only on these grounds. As for the Brahmanical temple situated outside the

[1] Vivien de Saint Martin is induced to locate the site of Pushkarāvatī much too low, at Nisatha, the present junction of the Swāt and Kābul-rūd (*Memoire*, p. 308). On the other hand Garrick seems tempted, as we shall see, to place it up stream a little too much to the north (*A. S. I.*, Vol. XIX, p. 100). We remain faithful to the middle view of Cunningham (*A. S. I.*, Vol. II, p. 30 and *Anc. Geog.*, p. 50) without claiming more than condensing his hypothesis and justifying it in detail (see the map, fig. 5).

[2] This is the popular and derivative meaning, the primary signification is, as is well known " place of sacrifice, " but the Prayāg *par excellence* of India owes its selection and consequently its name entirely to its position at the confluence of the Jumna and Ganges.

western gate, we cannot very well look for it, or for this gate either, anywhere else but at the end of the road by which the travellers used to come from the west, that is to say from Peshawar. In this case, the designation "south-west gate" would have been more accurate, but it is well known that everyday language does not affect such exactitude. Anyhow, at the south-west near the spot where the ferry boat of the old route still crosses the river, one sees a large mound exploited as usual by the villagers, but which by some extraordinary chance bears the half Indian name of Dharamsāl-Ḍhērī. "Dharamsāl," a Pathan explains to us, "is what we Mussalmans would call a mosque." Indeed it is thus that the Sikhs designate those buildings in which they preserve their Granth or sacred book. The term derived from the Sanskrit "*dharmaśālā*," is equivalent in their mouth to *devāyatana* or *mandir*. Thus, place and the name equally recall "the temple of the *deva*," whose idol performed so many miracles. It will be the task of the excavator to inform us further on the point. "To the east of the city" continues Hiuan-tsang, "is a *stūpa* built by Aśoka-raja." Unfortunately he omits to give us along with the direction, the dimensions and distances so that once more we can assert nothing definitely. We only know that, if we take the road to Shāhbāz-gaṛhi (Po-lu-sha) towards the east, we see on our right at less than a kilometre from the junction of this road with that of Swāt a low mound, which measures about a hundred metres in circumference. It is called by the name of "***Kanizaka***," which is given, we are told, to places where there is abundance of stones.[1] Above all, it is perfectly round, that is to say, it marks the site of an ancient ***stūpa*** of archaic form. Now this peculiarly ancient shape was the best, if not the only reason, that could be adduced at the time of Hiuan-tsang for attributing such and such a building to the good king Aśoka. Accordingly we are inclined to see in the Kanizaka-Ḍhērī the remains of the sanctuary mentioned by our author, the more so because the Kula-Ḍhērī, the only one which could claim this honour seems too irregular and, moreover, is placed too far to the north-east of the town. Hiuan-tsang is fortunately more explicit when he mentions "at five or six *li* to the north of the town" an old *Saṅghārāma* attached to a *stūpa* "several hundred feet high."[2] As soon as one passes the new bridge of boats to the north of Charsadda one sees at a distance of less than two kilometres the two mounds which he mentions. Both show the greatest resemblance to those of Shāh-jī-ki-ḍheri. They have for the same reasons the same composition, the same greyish colour, the same distorted appearance; only their position is reversed and their dimensions are considerably greater. The lower one to the east, is an immense quadrilateral of nearly 400 metres in length and 300 in width; the interior is nothing but a chaos with only the four corners still clearly marked. As for that to the west, it assumed the form of a square before the spoilers had encroached deeply upon the south-west corner; and though now it is but two hundred and fifty metres in length its ruined cliffs

---

[1] For all these sites see Fig. 5. Naturally all the freestone has been carefully removed but the mound is still covered with rounded boulders between which at the time of our visit, owing to the proximity of the new canal, the wheat was beginning to spring up.

[2]. The author of the biography of Hiuan-tsang says two hundred feet in height: but quite in accordance with his usual inexactitude he places the *stūpa* inside the *saṅghārāma* and the whole forty or fifty *li* to the north of the town. The translation of this hearsay text is not worth discussion.

still rise nearly thirty metres above the plain.[1] Such as they are, we must apparently recognise in them the remains of one of the ancient Buddhist foundations of the plains of Gandhāra : immense structures in which earth, bricks and water-worn pebbles play the principal part, and for that very reason very different from the convents which we shall meet with presently in the hills, where, on the contrary, stone was plentiful and space limited.

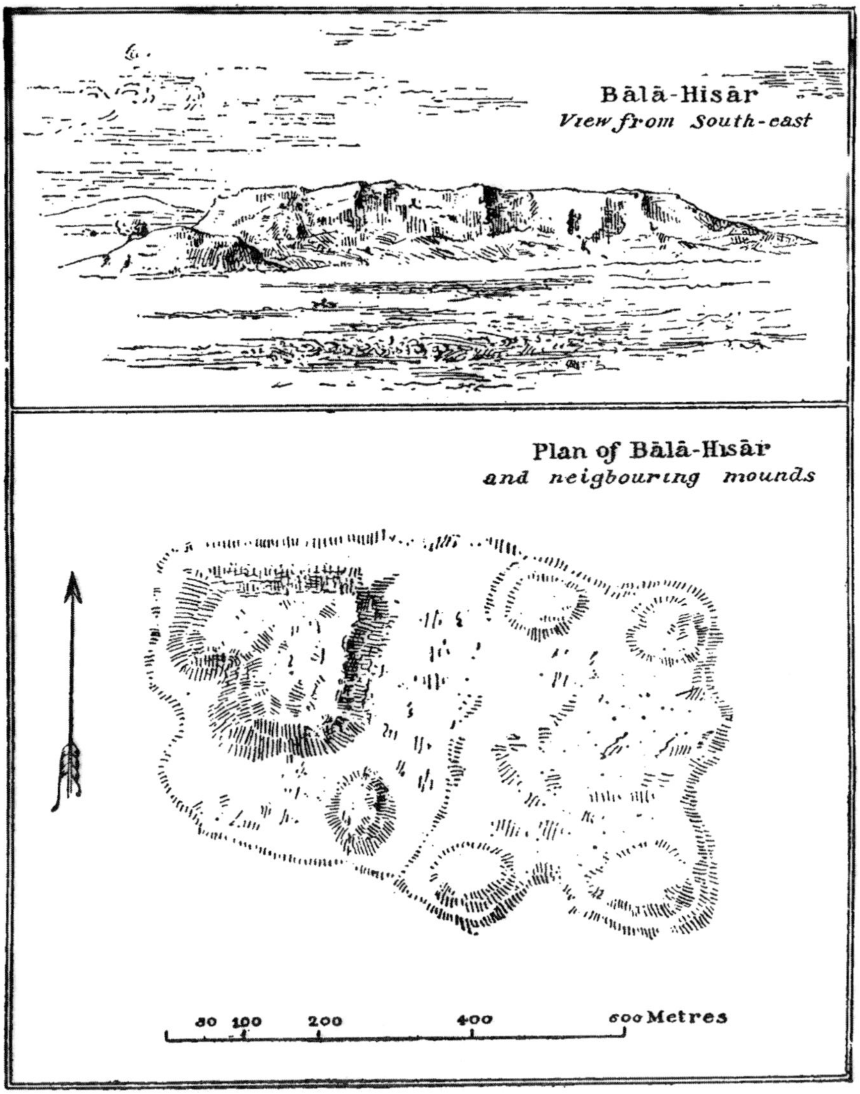

Fig. 6. Bālā Hisār (*Stūpa* of the Eye Gift ?).

[1] See the plan and the sketch, Fig. 6 (cf. *Sur la frontière indo-afghane,* Fig. 32). The outline of this tumulus resembles strangely that of the famous mound of Babil, on the site of Babylon, which is only ten metres higher (see Perrot and Chipiez, *Histoire de l' art dans l'antiquité,* Vol. 11, Fig. 37 and plate 1). The material of these mounds is very similar and they have been subject to the same destructive influences, internal collapse, the feeble resistance of their earthy mass to the inclemency of the weather, the exploitation of the materials by the neighbouring villages, etc. (cf. *ibid,* p. 133 and p. 154 n. 1).

We must not indeed neglect the mound to the east because that to the west is by far the most striking feature of the flat landscape, nor allow ourselves to be misled by the modern name of the latter—Bâlā Hisār—that is to say "the High Fort."[1] It is true that the Sikhs and the Durâni Sardars have in turn used this terraced height as a ready-made fortress and have even covered the summit with walls and structures in stone and unburnt brick, which are collapsing in their turn. But these ephemeral traces cannot deceive us as to the true nature of the imposing pile of ruins which they have for a moment turned to this transient use. One might just as well conclude from the fact that swarms of blue pigeons nest there, that it was originally meant for a dove-cote! We have here clearly the crumbling *débris* of one of those huge *stūpas* so common in the lower Swat valley. They were in fact little artificial hillocks formed of alternate layers of earth and of big round pebbles collected from the bed of the stream. Retaining walls restrained more or less the pressure of this confused mass of material and formed the facing of the terraces which rose in tiers to the dome. The whole was covered, by way of decoration, with wooden panels, slabs of marble and even with plates of precious metal. Of this very *stūpa* Fa-Hian states that it was at the time of his visit "adorned with silver and gold,"[2] Hiuan-tsang tells us simply that it was "made of carved wood and veined stone." Since that time, as at Shāh-jī-kī-ḍhērī, the wood has been completely destroyed by fire. The last freestones loaded into a boat close at hand are ready to be sold in the still thriving *bāzār* of Charsadda. Then the bricks are removed and finally the earth. Only the big round pebbles useless for building purposes roll down and pile themselves up scorned by all. But in places the walls, where now and then the bricks are blended with the stones, still exist. Elsewhere, where they have given way under the subsidence, they disclose the manner of construction by successive layers of earth and pebbles. Though the hillock is no longer, as twelve centuries ago, "several hundreds of feet high" it is nevertheless still a hundred or so. Mutilated and overthrown as it is, the huge pile will continue for a long time to discharge its original function, that is, to mark the spot where in a previous existence the Buddha gave his eyes in charity.

Thus the site, hitherto uncertain, of one of "the four great *stupas* of Northern India" has been determined, and we believe, convincingly.[3] That is the most im-

---

[1] This is precisely what has happened in the case of Mr. Garrick, the only archæologist or so called one who, as far as we know, has, up to the present concerned himself with the Bālā Hisār. To him it was nothing but a fortress except that he wished later to locate Pushkarāvatī there (*A. S. I.*, Vol. XIX, P. 100). To understand how he thought of perching a town which was more than a league in circumference on a terrace 250 metres square is a mystery. Let us remark in passing that the Bālā Hisār is a mile to the north of Charsadda and not "rather less than three miles to the west."

[2] Fa-hien Ch. X translation, Legge, p. 32. It will be noticed that Fa-hien makes Pushkarāvatī the capital of Gandhāra, and seems to be desirous of differentiating this latter country from "the kingdom of Purushapura" (Ch. XII translation, Legge, p. 33, translation, Beal, p. XXXII). So in the same way in his chapters VIII and IX he speaks successively of Udyāna and Swāt as if two different countries. This simply proves that the geographical nomenclature of Fa-hien is far from being impeccable and especially that it is infinitely less accurate than Hiuan-tsang's.

[3] According to Fa-hien (Ch. IX to XI) the four great *stūpas* commemorated the sacrifice or gift of the eyes, the head, the body and the flesh respectively. The second was at Takshaśila (near Shah-dheri), the third at Manikyala; as for the fourth which Hiuan-tsang very clearly locates in the hills which separate the district of Peshawar from Bunēr, Dr. Stein believes he has found it near the present village of Girarai (*Arch. Tour, etc.*, p. 92) and all the probabilities are in favour of this identification. On the other hand if we believe Dr. Stein, all that we can know of the first *stūpa*, that of the "Eye-gift" is, that it "lay somewhere in the central part of the Yusufzai plain." Cunningham on his part fancied he could locate it at Sahri-Bahlol (*A.S.I.* Vol. V, p. 45-6). It is strange that both these authorities should have forgotten the very categorical indication of Hiuan-tsang which is, moreover, in complete agreement with the evidence of Song-yun. Indeed the latter tells us (translation, Beal I., p.

portant point of all. Hiuan-tsang mentions, it is true, "two stone *stūpas*" at some distance to the east. The stones must have gone and how are we to find these two buildings already "in a ruinous condition" in the days of the pilgrim? However on the other side of the river and of the road to Swât in the area known as Pālāṭū there still exist two low round tumuli situated north and south, separated by a hundred metres and each about that width and evidently symmetrical. In that to the north a *banya* in search of stone, found a Buddha statue the pedestal of which has supplied one of the two so-called Hashtnagar inscriptions in Kharoshṭhī, and which the small Hindu community of the village of Rājaṛ have converted into an idol of Devī.[1] The workmanship and the magnificent polish of the sculpture give the most favourable idea of the artistic decoration of the monument which it formerly adorned. Can these two neighbouring mounds be the last vestige of the two *stūpas* "of Brahma and Sakra" of which even in their ruined state, Hiuan-tsang felt compelled to mention the twin beauty? At least their position less than two kilometres due east of the Bālā Hisār is another argument in their favour.

It seems, therefore, that with the aid of excavations it would be possible to recover the full complement of religious foundations on which Pushkarāvatī once prided itself.[2] These in their turn would help us to fix the exact circumference of the ancient town. We already know enough to assert that with "the crowded rows of houses" it was situated in the bend of the stream where we had, from the first, sought it, and which to judge by the very clear traces of the ancient bed, was in former days, a little narrower on the south side. In the interior of the city of which, moreover, Hiuan-tsang tells us nothing, we have nothing to note. The astonishing persistence of the ruins of the religious edifices is only equalled by the entire disappearance of secular habitations. These were, no doubt, as at present, only simple houses of mud or unburnt bricks. In these alluvial plains only, or almost only, religious monuments and, perhaps, royal palaces were in part constructed of stone, brought from afar, which has since found many a novel use. The number of *pakka* buildings, as in this country are called those built of rubble

---

CIII) that if, from the spot where Tathāgata plucked out his eyes to give them in charity, one crossed a large river and travelled sixty *li* towards the south-west, one came to Purushapura. In other words whilst Hiuan-tsang places "the *stūpa* of the Eye-gift" one stage to the north-east of Peshawar, Song-yun who travels in the opposite direction locates Peshawar one stage to the south-west of the same *stūpa*: that is both are unanimous in locating it at Pushkarāvatī.

[1] (Cf. *Sur la frontière indo-afghane*, p. 93). We have the details of this find from the very lips of the discoverer and we have been shown by him the spot whence it came. The really important point is, we believe, the pedestal which is now in the Lahore Museum and the inscription of which has been studied by Buhler and assigned by him to the time of Kanishka (*A new inscribed Græco-Buddhist Pedestal, Indian Antiquary* 1896, p. 311).

[The Rājaṛ pedestal is in the British Museum. The pedestal to which the learned author refers is one from the same neighbourhood and commonly designated the Charsadda pedestal. In reality it was found in or near the Mīr Ziārat mound on the Shahr-i-nāpursān site (cf. *Inscribed Gandhara Sculptures by Dr. J. Ph. Vogel, A. S. R.* 1903-4 p. 244 and *Græco-Roman influence on the Civilization of Ancient India by V. A. Smith, J. A. S. B.* 1889, p 144). *Translator*].

[2] The excavations carried out at Charsadda in the spring of 1903 by Dr. J. H. Marshall, C.I.E., and Dr. J. Ph. Vogel yielded nothing which could be adduced as evidence of the identification of the Bālā Hisār with the famous *stūpa* of the Eye-gift and, indeed, the explorers state their belief that the Bālā Hisār was nothing more than the Akropolis of the ancient city. That such a gigantic mass was not merely the site of even one of "the four great *stūpas* of Northern India" must be readily conceded, for the ruins of that reputed "the largest in Jumbudvipa" (the Kanishka chaitya) covered but a fraction of the area occupied by the Bālā Hisār. It must, however, be remembered that the excavations proved the existence of remains which appear to be Buddhist, and, being principally on the edges of the mound left all untouched a large area in the centre where might well have arisen the sought-for *stūpa*. There is, moreover, nothing inherently improbable in the supposition that on the Akropolis of Pushkarāvatī rose a famous religious monument; indeed, this would but render still more striking its resemblance to its more famous Athenian counterpart.

masonry and backed bricks, has always been extremely small compared to *kaccha* buildings, that is to say those simply made of sun-dried clay.

Another point which is worth considering is the exact meaning of the expression "fifty *li* or so" continually repeated in Hiuan-tsang's diary. Taken literally it corresponds to seventeen kilometres at the most. Now, from Peshawar to any point on the left bank of the River Swàt, one has to allow at least twenty kilometres. The sixty *li* given by Song-yun [1] would therefore be more exact if such rigorous accuracy were to be demanded in this matter. But Hiuan-tsang did not, for all we know, pace his route, he counted simply by stages for the simple reason he could not calculate it differently. "About fifty *li*" is the approximation which he regularly employs to designate the length of a day's march which, although very variable, was and still is, as an average, about four (Frenck) leagues, or ten miles. It is curious that the new English road which takes advantage of the strategic bridges built over the Kābul river puts about thirty kilometres between Peshawar and Charsadda which it approaches from the north : such, however, is the force of tradition that the official tariff reckons still only a single stage between the two towns although this stage already long, has been lengthened by a good third.

III.—From Pushkarāvati to Po-lu-sha.

At Pushkarāvatī our traveller quits the high road of India in order to make an excursion of two days to the north-west and to visit some *stūpas*, the merits of which he had heard extolled. Perhaps, even, he had been shown their tiers of umbrellas in the distance from the top of the highest terrace of the sanctuary of the "Eye Gift." To reach them, he had but to follow the road which then as now, ascends the still fertile and populous valley of the Swāt in the direction of Udyāna. The present road passes in ten miles no less than eight large villages (the "eight towns" which comprehend the common name of *Hashtnagar*) and is, all the way, lined with the *debris* of Buddhist convents and *stūpas*. Did Hiuan-tsang find them too numerous and the time too short to enquire, on his way, their names and their legends? Anyhow he tells us nothing of them. We must, from the outset, be content to remain unacquainted with the ancient name of the extensive ruins of Shahr-i-napursān near Rājar which cover several hectares and where one would be tempted to locate Pushkarāvatī were not the distance from Peshawar against this assumption. Besides at each step we are sure to meet similar ruins. There is the same silence regarding the neighbouring tumuli of Utmanzai and Turangzai and even that situated to the north of Umarzai, which bears at pre-

---

On the other hand the Mīr Ziārat mound where some authorities have located the site of the Eye-gift *stūpa* appeared to the explorers as unlikely to have been the site of such a famous monument as that described by Fa-Hien and Hiuan-tsang.

Dharmsāl Ḍhērī and Kanizaka Ḍhērī still await examination but Pālātū Ḍhērī was found to conceal the remains of what was apparently an ancient *stūpa* and its attendant monastery and Ghaz Ḍhērī the base of a *stūpa* from which a stone relic casket and reliquary were recovered by the fortunate explorers. It is, therefore, more than probable that the two mounds as suggested by M. Foucher mark, indeed, the two *stūpas* "of Brahma and Sakra" mentioned by the pious pilgrim as lying not far to the east of the *stūpa* of the Eye-gift (cf. *Excavations at Charsadda, A. S. I. 1902-3, pp. 141 ff* [*Translator*]).

[1] Translation, Beal, I, p. CIII. Moreover he reckons them from the right bank of the river already crossed. But this little difference is easily accounted for by the reasons given above. We do not any longer believe, in spite of what Cunningham thinks, that the least importance need be attached to the fact that the ever inaccurate *Biography of Hiuan-tsang* gives the number 100 *li* instead of the "50 *li* or thereabout" of the *Memoirs*. To do so would be to fall into worse extravagances.

sent the *ziārat* of Sahr-tor-Bābā and which in height yields only to the Bālā Hisār.[1] It is plain that our pilgrim has adopted the course of noting in his journal only the place where he made his daily halt at the end of his stage; and that is the *stūpa* about fifty *li* to the north-west named after "The Mother of the Demons." The Mother of the Demons (she had no less than five hundred sons) is more familiar to us under the name of Hāritī. It is not difficult to recognize in this child devouring Yakshī the personification of some infantile epidemic and the Buddhist counterpart of that Śītalā who receives even to-day the offerings and prayers of Hindu women. According to Mahāmahopādhyāya Haraprasād Shāstrī she is still worshipped in Nēpāl as the goddess of small-pox, for those strange goddesses, the terrors of mothers, are also their refuge. As stated in the *Bṛihat-Svayambhū-purāṇa*, each convent should contain a shrine of Hāritī. I-tsing tells us that her image was found under the porch or in a corner of the refectory of all the Buddhist monasteries of India. "She was represented with a child in her arms and three or four others around her knees." This mode of representing her disguised so well the horror of her true nature that she was invoked not only to cure sick children but also to bestow them on the childless.[2] Let us add that the Buddha, by an ingenious stratagem, managed to awaken in this terrible ogress more human feelings. He hid (some say under his alms-bowl) the best loved of her five hundred sons and as she wandered distractedly searching for him the Blessed One said: "Thou art heart-broken, because of one lost son among five hundred: how much more grieved must they be who by thy deeds have lost all their off-spring?" Thereupon she was immediately converted. How the conversion of the Yakshī, who ate the children of Rājgṛiha in Bengal came to take place at about sixteen kilometres to the north-west of Pushkarāvatī in the Punjab we need not investigate here. Besides, this will not be the only legend which originated in Central India and which we shall find acclimatized in Gandhāra by Buddhist missionaries. It will suffice if we succeed in locating the remains of the *stūpa* which was supposed, according to the testimony of Hiuan-tsang, to mark the site of this miracle. After having found so many ruins which he does not name, shall we not find at least the only one which he does mention?

Fig. 7. Hāritī.

---

[1] See *Sur la frontière indo-afghane*, Figs. 33-35.

[2] Cf. Haraprasad Śastri (*Discovery of living Buddhism in Bengal*, p. 19, and I-tsing, *Records of the Buddhist Religion*, translation, Takakusu, p. 37). I-tsing and Hiuan-tsang both agree as to her power of granting children. I-tsing also attributes to her that of bestowing wealth which she doubtless owed to her title of Yakshi and to the proximity usually of a statue of Mahākāla-Kubera. Fig. 7 from an original photograph shows a Græco-Buddhist statue of uncertain provenance now preserved in the British Museum (Height 0·80 m). It has also been published by Dr. J. Burgess (*Journal of Indian Art and Industry*, Vol. VIII, No. 62, pl. IV, 2).

Sure enough, in the direction and at the distance indicated, there is a vast mound which the English map calls Ḍhērī-Kāfirân, the "Mound of the Infidels," a name not without some value as it is still a memento. Nevertheless, it must be acknowledged that it produces only a weak argument in its favour.[1] Fortunately, however, the map is in error. From Sherpao to Tangi everyone will tell you that the term, more or less generic, of Ḍhērī-Kāfirān is applied to a low round mound—the remains of a *stūpa* again—situated by the side of the road, to the left, on leaving the village of Karawar. But the much more extensive tumulus, which is so called on the map, at two kilometres to the south-west of this same village is truly called *Sarē Makhē-ḍhērī*, and at once its identification with the Hāritī-*stūpa* becomes almost certain.

Let us listen to what the people of the neighbourhood have to say. From miles around when a child is attacked by "Red-face" (*Sarē-makh*, which seems to mean at the same time measles and small-pox) the parents are certain to bring it here: in the mouth of the little patient and in its *tāvīz* (the amulet holder, which hangs from its neck and which is of the same pattern as those of the Græco-Buddhist statues) is put a pinch of earth from the top of the mound and immediately it is cured. "Why?"—"Because it is so." The present inhabitants are incapable of giving the slightest semblance of a reason for this belief. Though the rite has been preserved, the legend has perished and they have not taken the trouble to invent another. It is not, as far as they know, by virtue of any *pīr* or Mussalman saint: there is no *ziārat* here. Moreover the place is as good for Hindu as for Pathān children: the mothers of both come here bringing as offerings grains of rice and wheat. In short we establish here a case, as rare in Gandhāra as it is common in Kashmir, where an old custom originally Indian has continued to be practised by Mussalmans until the present day. Perhaps here some particular reasons, such as the practical utility of the rite, the general belief of the Afghans in the healing powers of holy places and the want of orthodoxy of anxious mothers may serve to explain a survival so entirely exceptional in this country.

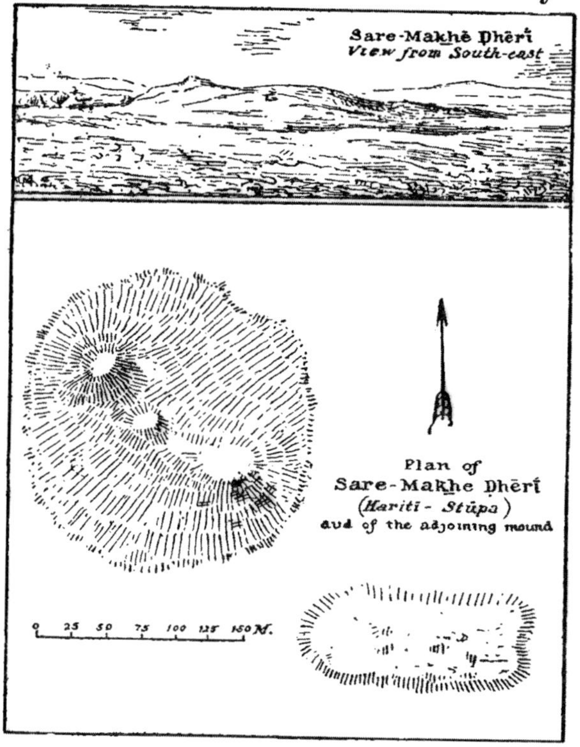

Fig. 8. Sarē-Makhē Ḍhērī (Hāritī *stūpa*).

[1] Colonel Deane (*loc. laud.*, p. 667) mentions this Ḍhērī Kāfirān as possibly representing the *stūpa* in question, but without other remark.

The *stūpa* was, moreover, extensive and its crumbled remains, round in shape, measure not less than six hundred metres in circumference. In places can be clearly distinguished the alternate layers of earth and boulders of which these enormous mounds were made. But the surface, very much broken, has disappeared everywhere under a litter of round stones, except at one prominent point at the north-west which is the spot still held sacred. This is where they come to take the miraculous earth and we found the summit strewn with grains of wheat according to a truly Buddhist rite, a traditional offering to a deity which even her worshippers no longer know. To the south-east another low *ḍhērī* of rectangular form, but of smaller dimensions (it is only seventy-five by hundred and fifty metres) marks, as usual, the site of the convent attached to the *stūpa*, probably that where Hiuan-tsang must have received hospitality more than twelve centuries ago.[1]

It still remains to recover the second *stūpa* which the pilgrim notes at the end of his second day's journey, and which commemorated another Indian legend

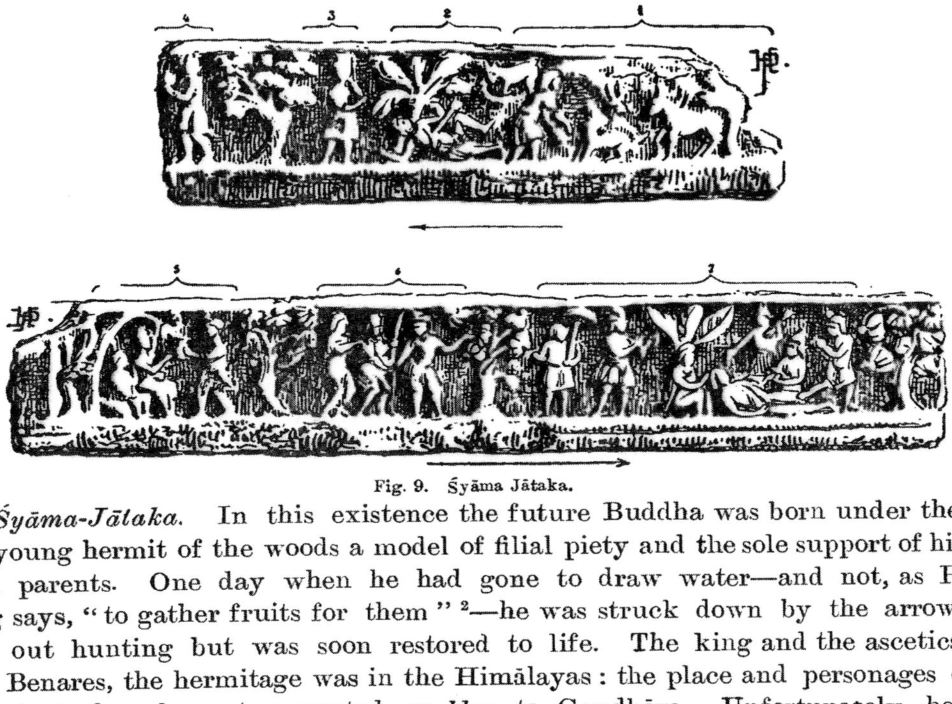

Fig. 9. Śyāma Jātaka.

the *Śyāma-Jātaka*. In this existence the future Buddha was born under the form of a young hermit of the woods a model of filial piety and the sole support of his aged blind parents. One day when he had gone to draw water—and not, as Hiuan-tsang says, "to gather fruits for them"[2]—he was struck down by the arrow of a king out hunting but was soon restored to life. The king and the ascetics were from Benares, the hermitage was in the Himālayas: the place and personages of the story had thus been transported *en bloc* to Gandhāra. Unfortunately, however pathetic this story may be, it scarcely lent itself to any practical application which had the chance of surviving. Although rather prolix on this subject, Hiuan-tsang is, on the other hand, very sparing in topographical data and states only that the second *stūpa* was "fifty *li* or so" to the north of the former. In fact, the route to Udyāna which up to that point ran towards the north-west following the valley,

[1] See the plan and the sketch on Fig. 8. For a view of the *stūpa* taken from the south-west cf. *Sur la frontière indo-afghane*, Fig. 36.

[2] At least the Pali version of the *Jātaka* (ed. Fausboll VI, p. 76) and that of the *Mahāvastu* (ed. Senart II, p. 212) agree on this point with the bas-relief from Sānchi (Fergusson, *Tree and Serpent Worship*, pl. XXXVI 1) and those from Jamāl-Gaṛhī. It is these latter which we reproduce (Fig. 9) from photographs preserved in the Calcutta Museum. The originals, now exhibited in the cases of the British Museum, formerly decorated the risers of a staircase which connected the

turns here northwards to avoid the wide loop formed by the river where it cuts a passage through the mountain barrier. It then leads straight through the pass of Spankarra towards the confluence of the Swāt and the Panjkora, the "Gouraios" of Alexander's historians. In this direction a road still crosses the barren plain, (the canals cannot reach so far), covered with stunted oleanders which may have given their name to the large village of Gandheri. It is probably in the vicinity of this village, which occupies an ancient site covered with ruins, that we must look for the *stūpa* in question.[1]

Now among the mounds of the neighbourhood there is only one which, from its size, answers to those which we have already seen and seems worth attention. It is found immediately to the east of the present village above the junction of the two torrents and measures a hundred metres in length by eighty in width.

It is accessible on the north side where the height is only thirty feet. On the side of the cliffs of the two ravines it reaches three times that height (Fig. 10). At the west a staircase descended to the water, perhaps as much an allusion to the tragic fate of Śyāma as for the convenience of the servants of the shrine. As usual, the *ḍhērī* is made half of earth, half of rounded pebbles from the torrents, and here also seems to have been utilized as a fortress. Its present name of Periāno-Ḍherī is due to the fact that it is supposed to be haunted by *peris*. To the south, the compass indicates exactly the south-south-east but the good Hiuan-tsang was content all his life with only the four cardinal and four intermediate points, one sees on the horizon the bizarre silhouette of the *stūpa* of Hāritī. It is about twelve kilometres as the crow flies, but at least three more kilometres must be allowed by road. May we conclude that *Periāno-Ḍhērī* represents the remains of the Śyāma *stūpa*? In the case of an isolated point as this,

Fig. 10. Periāno Ḍhērī (Śyāma-chaitya).

upper courts of the large convent of Jamāl-Gaṛhī. (Height 0·12 m.) The scenes represented unfold themselves along the sixteen steps in such a way that the eye followed them alternately from the right to the left and from the left to the right in boustrophedon: this we have indicated by arrows. In this particular instance we have to deal with the end of one riser and the beginning of another and we must read them one after the other, in these two ways. One sees in succession (1) Śyāma at the fountain in the midst of the tame deer; (2), the same struck by an arrow and fallen to the ground; (3), the king sorrowing over his mistake, then (4), catching up the young ascetic's water pot and (5) carrying it to the old blind parents; (6) that he may lead them to the corpse of the son; but (7) a god, holding in the left hand a thunderbolt and in the right a flask of ambrosia which with a curiously baptismal gesture he pours on Śyāma's head, restores him to life thus fittingly concluding the story. A portion only of these bas-reliefs has up to the present been published by Dr. Burgess (*loc. laud.* Pl. 23).

[1] Such is also the opinion of Colonel Deane (*loc. laud.*, p. 667) and he indicates to the north-east of Gandheri an interesting site where many beautiful sculptures have been found; but after visiting it we have been obliged to admit that these very small ruins cannot represent a large *stūpa* such as that for which we are searching. We pass for various reasons the *ḍhēris* of Kao-darra Tor-kot, etc. We regret our inability to obtain permission to visit the plain to the north of Gandheri because of the ill-disposed attitude of the people of Spankarra (cf. *Sur la frontière indo-afghane*, p. 198).

it appears to us, in the absence of any popular tradition, as impossible to affirm as to deny.

Fortunately, it so happens that the identification of this site is only interesting on its own account, and has no bearing at all on the further itinerary.[1] We can locate Po-lu-sha near Shāhbāz-gaṛhi as we shall see, from internal evidence. The only question which we have still to examine is as to the way by which Hiuan-tsang proceeded in four stages (about two hundred *li*) from a point near Gandheri to the present village of Shāhbāz-gaṛhī. Now it appears to us very difficult to admit that with his fondness for high roads (of which we are already aware), he should have started off, by short cuts in the direction of the south-east. If such an idea had occurred to him, the appearance of the barren plain, intersected at every step by deep and winding ravines, still almost deserted and unsafe, would have been sufficient to deter him from it. A much simpler course would present itself to him, that of returning by the same road. The two stages already travelled by him in a southerly direction brought him back to Pushkarāvatī; two more towards the east amply sufficed to cover the thirty-eight kilometres which separated Pushkarāvatī from Po-lu-sha; that is a total of four days' marching in the general direction of south-east.[2] We have scarcely any doubt, after examining the country, that he retraced his steps to rejoin the high-road of India about the point where he had left it. This road then, the same as to-day but more frequented, led through quite level country across the fertile fields which the canals (now re-opened), had not yet deserted. Then, as to-day, the circle of blue mountains closing in behind the traveller, stretched out endlessly to the right and left as if to limit the horizon. Only yonder towards the east they left in the sky-line a distant and faint gap which is the great gate of India the object of the pilgrim's yearnings. But Hiuan-tsang is not expansive: he does not, like Song-yun and I-tsing suddenly break out in poetical descriptions. We must take our companion as he is. In any case we shall find him again at the next large town.

IV.—Po-lu-sha.

We now purpose to prove the identification, already advanced by Cunningham, of Po-lu-sha with the site still partly occupied by the village of Shāhbāz-gaṛhī.[3] The proximity of the famous rock inscription of Aśoka would be of itself a proof of

---

[1] Colonel Deane maintains the contrary (*loc. laud.*, p. 668) and it is true that the fixing of this point would be very important if we had for the identification of Po-lu-sha no other information than knowing this town lay about 200 *li* to the south-east of the Śyâma *stūpa*. Happily we possess other indications, the uncertainty and contradictions of Vivien de Saint Martin and Cunningham showing very plainly the inadequacy of the former.

[2] The road from Pushkarâvatī to Po-lu-sha from Charsadda to Shâhbâz-gaṛhī was so easy that it was done in one stage. Song-yun reckons only one day between the two towns. So Fa-hien (translation, Beal, p. XXXI and translation, Legge, p. 32) counts only seven days between Pushkarâvatī and Takshaśila. Masson, in 1838, also travels from Peshawar to Shâhbâz-gaṛhī in two days sleeping the first night at Prāng (*Narrative of an excursion from Peshawar to Shāhbāz-gaṛhī* by C. Masson). At the present time one always goes straight on from Hoti-Mardan to Charsadda. But Hiuan-tsang seems to love short stages.

[3] See the map (Fig. 11). This is the second identification advanced by Cunningham: the first was Paloḍhērī (*A. S. I.*, Vol. II, p. 90 and *Ancient Geography*, p. 51). A visit made expressly to the village of this name has convinced us that the conjecture was in every respect untenable. It would never have been proposed by Cunningham or re-advanced by Colonel Deane (*loc. laud.*, p. 668) had it not been for the spell cast upon the imagination by the large cavern called the Kashmir Smats situated about 16 kilometres, by road, to the north-east of the village and in which delight is taken in recognizing, without any kind of investigation, the romantic retreat of the prince Viśvantara. (For the description of this magnificent cave cf. the article by Colonel Deane or *Sur la frontière indo-afghane*, p. 87*ff*.) The name Palo-ḍhērī in which Cunningham sought for traces of

the antiquity and importance of this place. The particulars handed down by Hiuan-tsang which can still be verified on the spot would be sufficient in their turn to identify it, not without great probability with Po-lu-sha. The still more precise details left in his account by Song-yun turn this probability almost to certainty.[1]

Of the town of Po-lu-sha (Varshapura) itself Hiuan-tsang tells us nothing.[2] Song-yun who had seen it in more prosperous times and who, having visited only the north-west of India, had leisure to launch out into details, is happily more loquacious. He praises in turn the fertility of the country, the coolness of its shady groves, the wealth and charm of the town, the number and exemplary morality of the inhabitants. His description alone would prove that we have here one of the four great cities lying along the important commercial road of Gandhāra.

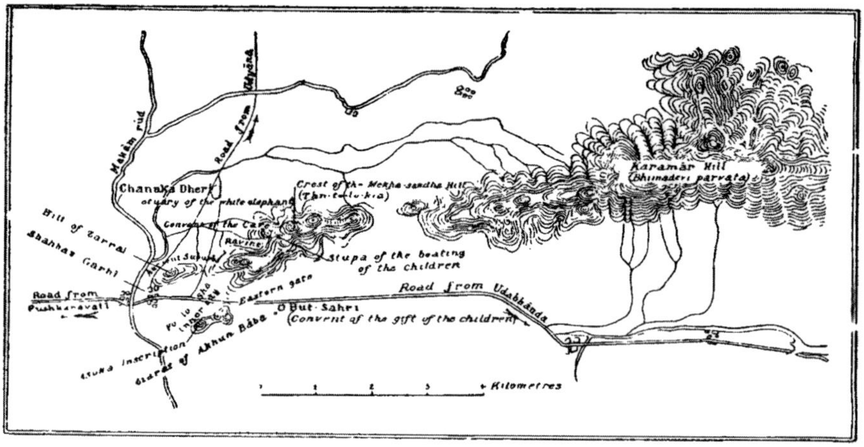

Fig. 11. Shābāz-gaṛhī (Po-lu-sha).

Now Hiuan-tsang who has forgotten to give us here that technical information

---

Po-lu-sha, is derived from some *palai* trees (palāśa, *butea frondosa*) which still exist near by as if to testify to what Mussalman improvidence can reduce a forest. As to the hypothesis that Po-lu-sha equals Shāhbāz-gaṛhī Cunningham sets it forth at length in the *A. S. I.*, Vol. V, p. 8 *et seq.* Against his demonstration we will bring forward no other objection than that it is slightly marred by an error and an omission : he is certainly mistaken as to the true situation of the prince's cave and moreover he has not recognized in Chanak-ḍhērī, which is incorrectly placed on his plan "the sanctuary of the white elephant." At the time of his visit to Shāhbāz-gaṛhī the existence of the ruins of the hill convent seem to have been unknown.

[1] Fa-hien who had descended from Swât to Purushapura by way of Pushkarāvatī and then travelled northwards towards Nagarabāra, reaching India eventually by way of Bannu, passed by neither Po-lu-sha nor Und and consequently does not mention them. We are, therefore, as regards the eastern portion of the Peshawar District limited to the memoirs of Hiuan-tsang and Song-yun. The very incoherent summary which has been preserved of the journeys of the latter and his companions—a kind of patchwork of different fragments of the accounts of Song-yun and Tao-yong, put together by a compiler and intermixed with details borrowed from Hoei-sang as the last phrase bears witness directs us regarding Po-lu-sha and its hill to two different places. The details concerning the sacred hill (which is located, however, very accurately with reference to the capital of Udɣāna, to 500 *li* south-west of Mangalapura) are given on the outward journey when leaving Udyāna (translation, Beal, p. XCVII). The pilgrims scarcely went beyond Takshaśila and the description of the town places it in the course of their return journey which brings them back towards the west from Takshaśila to the Indus in three days and three more days (thirteen is a mere slip on the part of Beal) from the Indus to Po-lu-sha which they call Fo-cha (translation, Beal, p. CII). It would be worth while publishing a new edition of this confused text, the sense of which has not always been satisfactorily realized by Beal. Thus he takes the Swāt for the Indus (CII, note 58) already crossed on the preceding page and he has, as we shall see, quite misunderstood the story of the asses on the hill. Nevertheless he has certainly recognized in the Fo-cha of Song-yun the Po-lu-sha of Hiuan-tsang.

[2] We disclaim all idea of giving the name of this town in its original form. Stan. Julien proposes Varusha which is hardly satisfactory. Varshapura would be better and seems confirmed by Song-yun's transcription which has only two syllables Fo-sha (in Fo-sha-fu, the third syllable *fu* or *pu* represents the first part of the word *pura*, city) ; but on the other hand Hiuan-tsang's usually correct notation is opposed to it. This is but another example of the difficulty experienced in recognizing an Indian word in its Chinese transformation when we have not the assistance of some Sanskrit text.

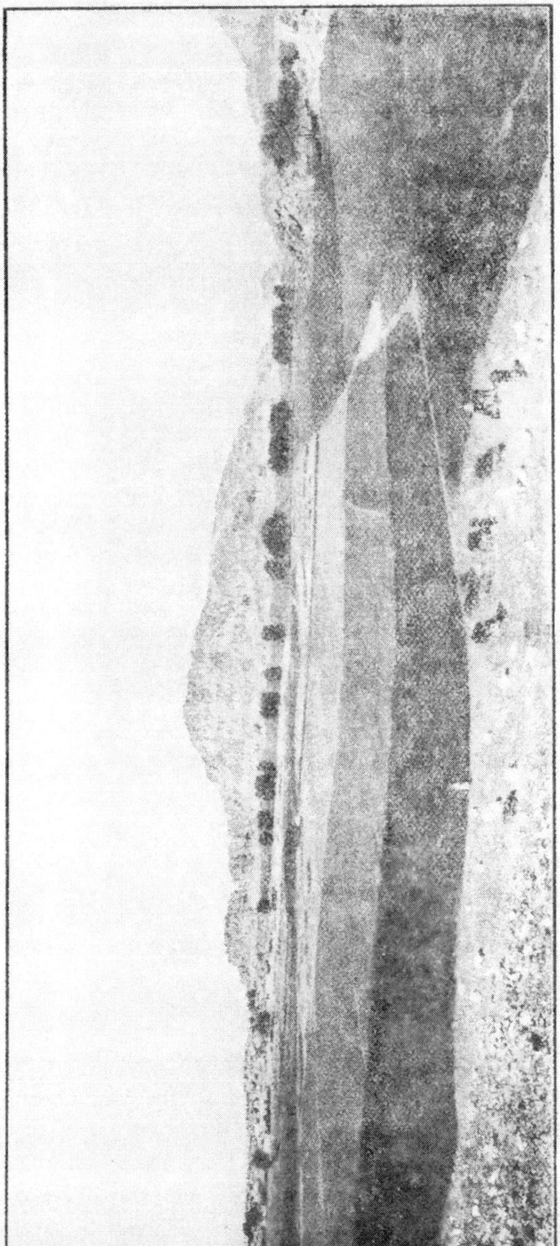

Fig. 12. Shāhbāz-garhi from the south. Aśoka inscription on extreme right.

estimates the circuit of Purushapura at forty *li*, that of Pushkarāvatī at fifteen, that of Udabhānda at twenty. If we now consult the map, we cannot help noticing that the little triangle of hills, of which the village of Shāhbāz-gaṛhī occupies the north-west angle, was too confined to have ever held a large town, had it been even only fifteen *li* or five kilometres in circumference. We must therefore admit that Po-lu-sha spread beyond its circle of hills. At the same time we can better understand what Song-yun tells us of "the excellent disposition of the outer and inner rampart" or "of the town and the suburbs."[1] If the city had remained enclosed within its natural defences, it would not have required that line of "exterior walls" which Hiuan-tsang describes on the north side. It is also possible

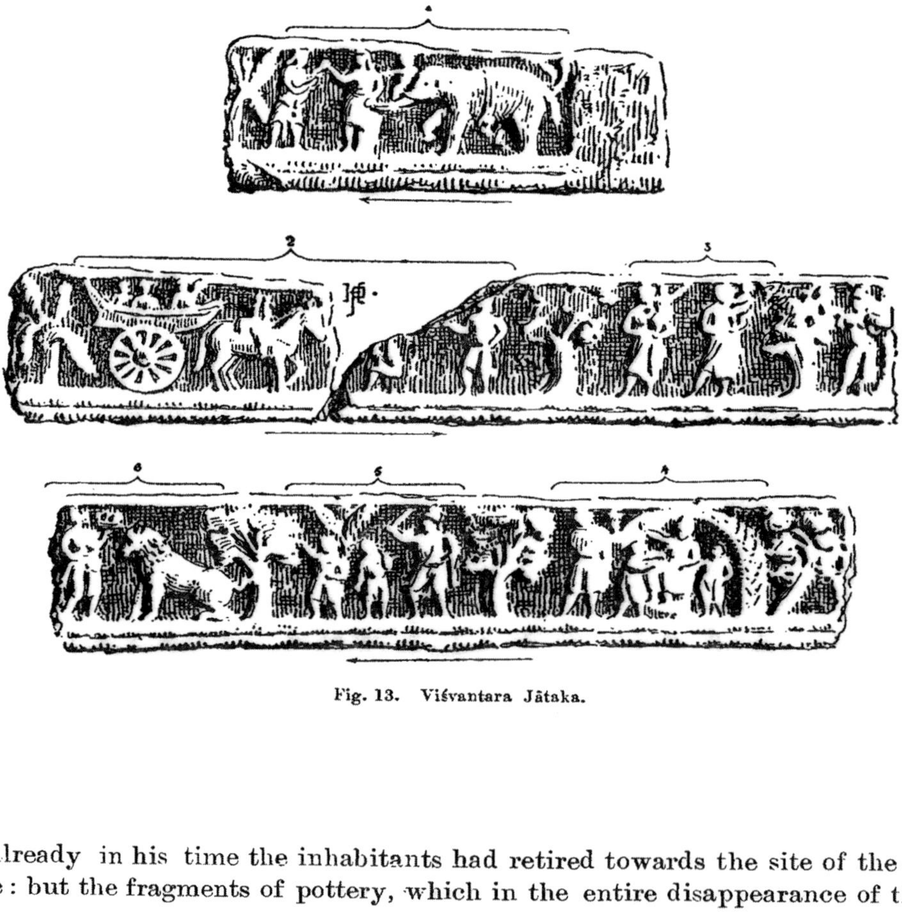

Fig. 13. Viśvantara Jātaka.

that already in his time the inhabitants had retired towards the site of the present village: but the fragments of pottery, which in the entire disappearance of the mud

---

[1] After a manuscript translation by M. E. Chavannes who has kindly re-examined the passage for us. The translation which Beal gives of this passage "The city walls have gate-defences" is entirely inadequate. For a panoramic view of Shāhbāz-garhī taken from the south, see Fig. 12 and *Sur la frontière indo-afghane*, Fig. 11.

houses remain the sole witnesses of the ancient habitations, continue as far as five hundred metres and more to the north of the little hill of Zarrai, to mark the site of the "suburbs" of Po-lu-sha.

The principal interest of the town in the eyes of the pilgrims and of archæologists, is, that, somehow or other, it had become the seat of the most celebrated of the *Jātakas*. It is well known how in the course of his penultimate existence the future Buddha born a princely heir in a royal family under the name of Viśvantara had realized on earth the perfection of charity. To begin with, he went so far as to give to some Brahman strangers a miraculous white elephant which had the power of producing rain at will, and which was a state treasure (Fig. 13). Banished from his country for this act more generous than diplomatic, he then gave in alms even on the road to exile his horses and his chariot. Finally a wicked Brahman and the king of the Gods succeeded in finding him in his solitude and obtained from him his two children and even his wife![1] It needs, if we may believe the legend, no less sacrifice to become a Buddha. That which concerns us here is that of all the religious foundations which were in the neighbourhood of Po-lu-sha, there was none which did not recall some episode of this edifying tale and was not supposed to mark the scene thereof.

Hiuan-tsang alone mentions the *stūpa* and *saṅghārāma*—the two always go together—which were found "outside the eastern gate of the town." A narrow rocky defile, enclosed between the hills, is the only access to Po-lu-sha on the east. It is surely not pure accident that less than a kilometre beyond, on the right of the main road to Und (Udabhāṇḍa) we meet with the large mound of But-Sahri. Being close to the Ziārat of *Akhun-Bābā* and covered with Mahommedan tombs this mound has up to the present escaped excavation, but its name sufficiently indicates its Buddhist origin. The monks which Hiuan-tsang met there, to the number of about fifty, were unanimous in assuring him that it was at this very place that the prince had given his two children to the Brahman.[2] To the north of the town, however, was to be found the most important sanctuary which Hiuan-tsang and Song-yun agree in mentioning first of all. To reach it one had, according to the former, to pass not only the natural gate which opened on this side between the hills but also that of the second enclosure formed by the outer walls; that is the reason why Song-yun reckons for the journey from the suburbs and gardens only one *li*. He describes minutely the magnificence of the temple, the number and great beauty of the stone images "covered with gold leaf" and the deep impression which the touching representation of the legend produced even upon the barbarous *Hou* (Tartars ?). He lays particular stress upon the sacred tree which

---

[1] We reproduce (Fig. 13) some scenes from this legend after the bas-reliefs from the same staircase at Jamālgaṛhī which has already given us Fig. 9. We see here the prince Viśvantara (1) giving the royal elephant, then (2) his chariot and his horses, and (3) continuing his journey on foot with his wife, each of them carrying one of the children; on the 3rd fragment (4) the prince gives his two children to the wicked Brahman who (5) beating them leads them away whilst (6) Madrī who returns from the gathering of fruits is stopped by Śakra disguised as a lion. Here again we avail ourselves of photographs from the Calcutta Museum; the original is likewise in the British Museum. (Cf. *Burgess loc. laud.*, pl. 23 and *Anc. Mon. of India*, Pl. 151.)

[2] Stan. Julien and Beal agree in translating "that he sold them." According to his translators it is an error of Hiuan-tsang. A view of But-sahri will be found in the foreground of Fig. 7, of *Sur la frontière indo-afghane.*

stood before the shrine and from which, he tells us, it derived its origin and its name for the legendary white elephant was said to have been tied to it. According to a common saying, the law of Buddha and this tree would perish at the same time: but the latter must have died a little too soon, for Hiuan-tsang does not seem to have known it: the "temple of the white elephant" of Song-yun is for him nothing but the spot where the exiled prince had taken final leave of the friends who had accompanied him to the outside of the city. Be that as it may, we have not a shadow of a doubt that in the direction and at the distance indicated the mounds of Chanaka-Ḍhērī, and they alone, are worthy of representing the remains of this important foundation.[1] It may even be asked whether the term Chanaka-Ḍhērī, which has no meaning in Pushtu and which is the regular equivalent of the Sanskrit *Kanaka-Chaitya*, the "golden sanctuary" does not still recall the "dazzling spectacle for human eyes" which presented itself to Song-yun: at any rate the existence of a *stūpa* of this name in Gandhāra is attested for elsewhere.[2] Systematic excavations would without doubt yield, if not new evidence for the identification of Po-lu-sha, at least sculptures not less interesting than those already obtained from the neighbouring hill.

This hill is the third point mentioned by Hiuan-tsang. "To the north-east of Po-lu-sha city about 20 *li* or so we come," he tells us, "to Mount Tan-to-la-kia."[3] On the way to Chanaka-Ḍhērī, we cannot help noticing the hill in question rising up before us. It now bears the name of Mēkha-sanda, which means "the female and male buffalo," in Sanskrit *Mahishī-shaṇḍau*.

Here again it might be supposed that, granted the well known meaning of *Mahishī* (queen or princess) this Indian name may contain a distant allusion to the supposed sojourn of Prince Viśvantara and Madrī his faithful wife. But a more convincing proof in support of our identification will be to find as easily as in the

---

[1] See the map (Fig. 11) Stan. Julien goes so far as to translate that near to the *stūpa* there were "about a hundred convents." Beal understands that there was a convent with some hundred monks which is more reasonable.

[2] We have already noted above that *ḍhērī* is equivalent to *chaitya*; as for Chanaka it is, according to Pathan usage the regular change for Kanaka. Regarding the authenticity of the Nepalese miniature which, as the inscription bears evidence, claims to represent "the golden sanctuary of the Peshawar District, Northern India," (*Uttarapathē Purushapura-maṇḍalē Śrī-kanaka-chaityah*), we are compelled to refer to our *Étude sur l'Iconographie bouddhique de l'Inde* (pp. 54 and 59). Colonel Deane has had in his hands one of those stone statues covered with golden plates of which Song-yun speaks (*loc. laud.*, p. 660).

[3] Here again we abandon the idea of restoring the Sanskrit name. In their genius for transforming foreign words the Chinese have finished by bewildering themselves. On one hand Tan-to may represent *danta* and *su-danta* "with beautiful teeth," one of the names of prince Viśvantara; this word in its turn is perhaps only an error for *Chan-tche* (literally "illustrious resolution" equalling Sudānta (the well disciplined, the self-controlled) which is given to the prince as well as to the hill by Song-yun and which Beal proposes to alter to "*Chan-che*" "illustrious charity," Sudāna. Nevertheless M. E. Chevannes informs us that the reading rejected by Beal is established by the texts so that one is tempted to reduce the two transcriptions of Hiuan-tsang and Song-yun to an original and unique Dānta or Sudānta-lōka. But on the other hand M. Sylvain Levi in a lengthy note to his interesting article on the *Missions de Wang Hiuan Ts'e dans l'Inde* (*Journ. Asiat.*, mars-avril 1900, p. 304) observes that °*lokia* is the regular equivalent of °*laka*, whilst *T'an-to*, *Tan-to* or *Tan-te* (for all three forms are met with) may correspond to *daṇḍa*': he ingeniously puts together the name of Daṇḍa-piṅgala a city in Northern India according to the geographical lists of the Bṛihatsaṁhitā. Let us moreover mention that the Chinese commentator's translation of *Tan-to* by "shaded" seems to require *daṇḍa* in the sense of "stem" or branch and that Daṇḍa-piṅgalaka would allude to the russet colour (piṅgala) ascribed by the pilgrims to the trees on the hill; thus would be formed again Daṇḍarakta or Daṇḍālakta. Is another conjecture desired? Daṇḍālaka (à la chevelure de branchages) would no less explain itself by the descriptions of the pilgrims and would have the advantage of doing no violence to the Chinese transcription; but it must be confessed that the sense would be a little forced; one might then consider Daṇḍaka as recalling the name of the forest which was the scene of the exile of Rāma, etc. One realizes perfectly that only a conclusive Sanskrit text would be able to put an end to our uncertainty.

previous case on the slopes of the little mountain, the cave and the two *stūpas* which Hiuan-tsang describes.

"On the mountain there is a stone chamber where the prince and his wife dwelt and practised meditation." There is many a natural shelter thus formed in the rocks which stud the hill, and we should be not a little embarrassed in making a choice, were it not that Song-yun had come to our aid and restricted our quest: "To the south-east of the crest of the hill is the rock cave of the prince." Here, indeed, half way up the hill of Mēkha-Sanda, there is a hollowed rock whither the two half ruined foot-paths, the one ascending from Shāhbāz-gaṛhi and the other from Chanaka-Ḍhérī, directly lead. Setting out from the town by the northern gate, Song-yun believed, and for a long time we believed the same, that he was ascending the southern slope and finding his grotto on his right hand he concluded that it was at the south-east of the crest: and such indeed is the relative position of these two points to the eyes of the visitor coming from Po-lu-sha. Only when tracing out the data of Song-yun on the large scale English map we become aware of our common mistake. In reality, the little ridge runs east and west but the rounded slope faces more to the west than to the south. One has to yield to the superior precision of topographers. The pilgrim and we also, had made in all the bearings he gives, a constant error of nearly 90 degrees in the same direction.[1] The cave is in reality to the west-south-west and not to the south-east of the highest peak. Fortunately we possess not less than three further proofs of its authenticity.

First of all Song-yun testifies to the existence of two chambers in the same cave. This detail is not without interest. It is indeed definitely stated in the versions which we possess of the *Jātaka* and it is repeated by our pilgrims that Viśvantara and Madrī in their retreat practised a life of asceticism. Now to refrain from cohabitation was an invariable rule of *vanaprasthas* or hermits. In the same way we find for example on the bas-reliefs of Sānchi the father and mother of Śyāma each sitting by their respective doors. The representation of the *Viśvantara-Jātaka* on the first architrave of the north gate displays likewise two huts of leaves and it is definitely stated in the Pāli text that the prince and princess had each their *parnaśālā*.[2] In Gandhāra, therefore, were shown, under one rock it is true, the two adjoining but distinct "stone chambers" where they were supposed to have lived in the most edifying manner: the monks who spread the legend had known how to select their *mise en scène*. Since then the rock seems to have suffered much from the ravages of time and the two stone cells, which could never have been very spacious, are partially choked with *débris*. Nevertheless, in the course of our researches, we have had occasion to ascertain that ten persons can take shelter from rain in the single recess to the left. The dwelling was, therefore, adequate for the royal hermit, its very straitness affording an additional ground for edification.

---

[1] The very persistence of this error removes all the uncertainty it might throw upon the rest of our identifications. Thus the site of the beating of the children which Song-yun believed to be to the north-east of the cave is in reality to the south-east so the search for the leafy hut (parṇaśālā) of the prince and the place where Madrī was detained by the lion, which he places to the south and west respectively of the cave must be made to the west in the case of the former, and in the case of the latter to the north. In short all the indications of Song-yun hold good: in order to find one's way according to the orientation adopted by him it is sufficient to turn the map a quarter of a circle or of substituting in one's mind the east for the north.

[2] Cf. above p. 19 and n. 2; see *Anc. Mon. of India*, Pl. XLV. Cf. the Sanskrit version of the *Jātakamālā* translation, Speyer, p. 83, and for the Pāli Fausboll, Vol. VI p. 520 and 541.

Fig. 14. Hill of Viśvantara. The double cave, walls and adjacent shrine.

In the second place Song-yun states "Ten paces in front of this cave, is a great square stone on which it is said that the prince was accustomed to sit; above this Aśoka raised a memorial tower." It is the *stūpa* which Hiuan-tsang in his turn mentions as having been "built by Aśoka at the spot where the prince dwelt in solitude." Even as one would anticipate this building, already regarded as very ancient twelve centuries ago, has collapsed and its *débris* has been carried away by the rain on these steep slopes; nevertheless, about ten metres from the cave and to its left (it must not be forgotten that the Chinese pace is double) we believe we still strike the remains of its substructures. This is a line of enormous stones almost unhewn which formed the foundation of one of those walls of which we have met several better preserved specimens on the hill and which undoubtedly are in point of construction, the most ancient of the existing remains. Indeed nothing is more archaic than their structure: it could best be described as a pile of huge blocks of stone scarcely dressed but nevertheless carefully fitted and occasionally finding in the natural rock an immovable bed.

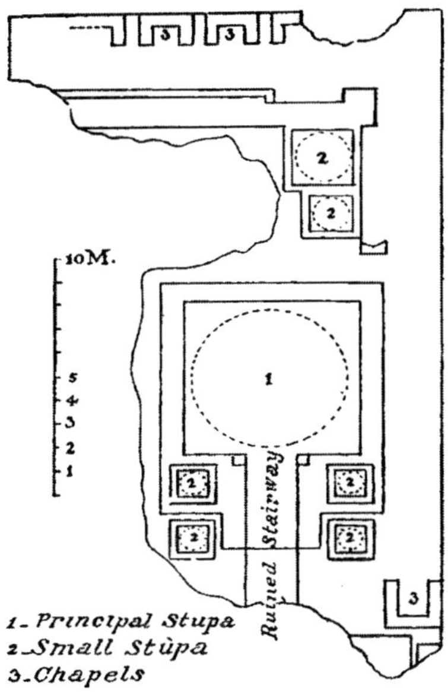

Fig. 15. Plan of the *stūpa* near the cave.

The exterior face is more or less dressed and presents that arrangement known as "polygonal dressing." Their evident purpose on the slopes of the little mountain was to serve as a retaining wall to a terrace; this in its turn formed the artificial platform for those *stūpas* which are now so completely destroyed that were it not for the cyclopean nature of their substructures, not a trace of them could have been recognized.

These walls form a marked contrast to those of the court of the *stūpa* and chapel which are contiguous with the double cave and definitely prove its sanctity. The latter are built in the ordinary style of Græco-Buddhist edifices by regular layers of irregular blocks, the interstices of which are filled with small flat stones which rectify all the inequalities. The whole surface was then covered with a layer of stucco set off by ornaments and figurines in relief, statues in stone or stucco of excellent workmanship completing the decoration.[1] This group of votive monuments necessarily pre-supposes the existence on the hill of a convent connected therewith: Song-yun estimates the number of its monks at two hundred; perhaps it was nearly deserted in the time of Hiuan-tsang who is silent on the point. Chapels and *stūpa*, although half demolished, owe their comparative preservation to the fact that they occupied the narrow top of a spur which had been previously levelled. It cannot be doubted that they together with the cave and "Aśoka's

[1] Some ten years ago this sanctuary was the object of excavations which according to the people of the place were very fruitful but of which, as far as we know, no account has been published. During the summary but methodical clearance which we had to carry out in order to draw the plan of the principal *stūpa* (Fig. 15) we disclosed the pilasters of its base and a certain number of sculptures in stone and stucco which had escaped the first excavators and which are now in the Louvre Museum [see *Sculptures greco-bouddhiques* (Musée du Louvre) in *Monuments and Mémoires*, Vol. VII with two plates one of which probably represents an image of the Bodhisattva Viśvantara].

stūpa" marked the principal station of the pilgrimage to the hill and from this centre start all Song-yun's other indications.

Is any further proof wanted ? On the hill was still shown the spot where the wicked Brahman had beaten the two children, the boy and the girl, who refused to follow him. Song-yun had even seen the tree round which they had run to escape from their persecutor. At the spot where their blood had flowed under the rod, rose a *stūpa* which Hiuan-tsang carelessly states "was by the side of and at a little distance from the other." Here again Song-yun deserves well of archæologists when he fixes the site of it by reference to the former—"one *li* to the north-east, fifty paces lower down the mountain." In the direction indicated by the pilgrim—that is to say on the right looking towards the summit of the hill, really south-east according to the map,[1]—we are indeed led, in descending the slope obliquely, to the ruined foundations of a terrace built, like the one just mentioned, of blocks of stone, but better preserved. There must the *stūpa* have been. Even the reddish hue which the monks pointed out to the pious credulity of the pilgrims still clings to the stones, rain especially giving them the forbidding colour of coagulated blood, the blood with which the children, so they said, had reddened the earth. But that which definitely determines the exact spot is what Song-yun adds that of this holy blood a spring had birth. And, indeed, his indications take us to the centre of the higher basin of the ravine, the very spot where a spring, in the time when there were springs, must naturally have gushed out, however miraculous it was supposed to be.

It would be idle to indulge any longer the petty archæological game of seeking on one of the projections of the spur of the cave "the leafy hut of the prince" or along the footpath which leads to Chanaka-Ḍhērī the claw marks of the God Śakra when, in the guise of a lion, he kept the princess away from the hermitage. It seems to us equally superfluous to investigate to-day, which of the caves on the hill could in former days have best served as the asylum of the Rishi Uh-po whose miracles Song-yun relates and who—just like the famous *sannyāsī* Bhāskarācarya who has recently died in Benares—had his temple and image erected during his lifetime by the rājas of the country. We should, also have only to choose between the numerous pieces of wall with which the whole of the slope facing Shāhbāz-gaṛhī is strewn, to discover the retreat of the anchorite Achyuta or the temple of Samantabhadra close to the summit and so on. It is enough that we have been able to profit by the agreement of the evidence to identify, besides the hill itself, the principal sites consecrated by local tradition to the memory of Viśvantara which our pilgrims were content to repeat with such docility.

Upon the whole their curiosity had ample reason to be satisfied. The *mise en scène* of the Jātaka was, as one sees, quite complete and most cleverly arranged. What doubt could there be, after so many palpable proofs, that this spot was the cradle of both the prince and the legend ? Carping criticism might, indeed, have asked how after having parted with the white elephant at the north of the town, the

---

[1] See Fig. 11 and 14. The base of the "*stūpa* of the flogging of the children" is on the right of the ridge which bears "The sanctuary of the cave," at the head of the formerly well-wooded ravine. The view of Fig. 14, 4 is taken precisely from this very base looking towards the north-west.

prince was able near the east gate to give away the children whom the Brahman then flogged on the hill. But the difficulty is not insurmountable: with a little good-will all is easily accounted for. Above all, everybody must live and between the three great Buddhist convents of Po-lu-sha, that of the north, that of the east gate and the one on the hill, it was only fitting that there should be no jealousy. Moreover the exile of the prince was purely theoretical and from his improvised solitude he was able to gaze upon his native city almost at his feet. But a convent should not be too remote from the city which it sanctified and on which it subsisted. "Neither too far from the town nor too near" such is the precept of the sacred texts, for if too close a proximity was likely to have annoying consequences, an excessive distance would have been too inconvenient for both the *bhikshu* and the *upāsaka*, for the monks as well as for the faithful laity.

But it will perhaps be asked, where are those woods that Hiuan-tsang describes and in which the prince wandered under bowers of verdure? Where is that enchanting and flowery landscape, peopled with birds and butterflies, the charm of which made Song-yun so homesick and to which the local monks did not hesitate to apply the descriptions of the holy books?[1] We are shown only a bare plain and still more barren hills. It is true, shade and gardens have long ago disappeared together with the water which gave them life but it is certain that formerly springs flowed in these ravines now dry except when short-lived torrents sweep down them after rain. The collection of human beings to be conjectured from the buildings with which the hill-side was covered would be quite a sufficient reason, if the pilgrims did not state definitely that it was so. Song-yun does not omit to mention "the fountain which supplied the prince with water." Not content with thus settling in passing the question of water, he informs us also on the mode of provisioning the numerous monks who inhabited the hill. These had, it seems, finally found their daily journey in quest of food in the bazars of the town too fatiguing and like the Tibetan lamas were fain to confine themselves in their monastery; but their food was, nevertheless, miraculously supplied. "The food is always carried to the top of the mountain by a number of asses. No man drives them, they come and go of their own accord. They set out between three and four in the morning and arrive about noon: they always arrive in time for the midday meal."[2] The detail is of importance; for let us suppose a delay on the part of the asses, and the monks who were forbidden by their order to eat after midday, would have been obliged to fast until the morrow. So the pious descriptions of our travellers call up even in the smallest detail, in the midst of its dried up frame, the life of this holy hill formerly as swarming with monks and pilgrims, if not as thickly covered with shrines, as are, thanks to the preserving devotion of the Jains, those of Palitana

[1] We cannot resist the pleasure of quoting this beautiful passage of Song-yun, according to the translation which has been very kindly communicated to us by our friend M. Ed. Chevannes. "Of the pleasant fountains and delicious fruits, obtained on the hill one may read the description in the sacred books, *sūtras*, and legends. Its valleys are agreeably warm, its trees remain green even in winter. On the occasion (of our visit) it was the first month of the year, a soft breeze fanned us, the birds sang in the vernal trees, and the butterflies flitted over the beds of flowers. Song-yun felt himself alone in a distant land, and whilst he gave himself up to the contemplation of this lovely landscape, thoughts of return and regret completely absorbed his mind: he was attacked by an old fever which seized and weakened him for a whole month. Thanks to the charms of a Brahman he recovered his health."

[2] Translation, Ed. Chevannes: Beal has entirely misunderstood this passage of Song-yun which is also found in the Si-iu-tchi (cf. S. Levi, *loc. laud.*, *Journ.-Asiat.*, mars-avril 1900, p. 324).

or Parisnāth at the present time. One feels how the identification borrows certainty from this constant agreement of texts and places: the topographical data which we have yet to examine will still further confirm it.

V.—From Po-lu-sha to Udabhāṇḍa.

Before continuing his journey towards Udabhāṇḍa Hiuan-tsang tells us of an excursion in the direction of Udyāna as had been the case at Pushkarāvatī. Did he make it at this very time, going and returning by the same route? Or did he travel this road only in the course of those wanderings between the district of Peshawar, Būner and Swāt of which the account he has left us of Udyāna bears evident traces, and has he when finally arranging his chapters, simply recorded here this portion of his itinerary as relating to Gandhāra? We do not pretend to decide this point. The important thing is that there can be no doubt as to the route he indicates: it is that which ascended from Po-lu-sha to Swāt by the Shahkote Pass, the *Hathi-lār* or "elephant defile" of the present inhabitants and the most important pass of these mountains, before the English in 1895 chose the Malakand route as their strategic road to Chitrāl.

On this other road to Udyāna, Hiuan-tsang travelled from Po-lu-sha to the north-west "about 100 *li*" that is to say two stages, exactly as he had done to the north-west of Pushkarāvatī. This road led him by the ancient sites of Bakshali and Saval-Ḍhēr, but he simply states that he "crossed a small hill" without doubt at the spot where the Sanavar or Pāja chain abruptly sinks down, throwing off into the plain that line of isolated hills which runs from Jamāl-Gaṛhī to Takht-i-Bāhī. He had on his left, the now famous ruins of Jamāl-Gaṛhī, and on his right those of Sikri or Shikar-Tangai (the valley of the chase), and of Tarelli brought to notice by Colonel Deane. The halting place itself must have been immediately to the north of the hills at the spot where extensive stretches of stones mark the site of a large village. But Hiuan-tsang mentions neither the halting place nor the neighbouring monasteries. His silence regarding the latter compels us to believe that they were among those abandoned convents already "filled with wild shrubs," which, by his own confession, were in the majority in this country: otherwise he could never have resisted the temptation of going there to count the monks and to make them talk.

After crossing the Pāja chain, the road to Udyāna turns straight towards the north a circumstance which our traveller has failed to note, perhaps because it seemed to him quite sufficient to give the initial direction, or it may be that having lost sight of Po-lu-sha behind the curtain of mountains, he was no longer conscious of the exact direction of his route with regard to that point. There is no doubt that the "large mountain" which he presently saw before him was the high grey wall of Swāt. The second stage led him as far as the foot of the southern slope of that chain. There, near a *stūpa* attributed to Aśoka rose a monastery which had appropriated the rather vulgar legend of the Rishi Unicorn (Ekaśringa).

Hiuan-tsang repeats without a frown, how the holy man after many years of austerities allowed himself to be seduced by a courtesan to such a degree that she made him carry her astride on his shoulders even to the King's court. One recognizes in this tale an early version of the "lay of Aristotle" and the fables which our mediæval Bestiaries relate concerning the unicorn : and indeed it had not been invented by the monks who derived their income from it. As to their convent "to the south of the mountain" Colonel Deane thinks, with considerable reason, that it must be sought for above the village of Palai near the mouth of the great pass.[1] Unfortunately, having been able to visit only the northern slopes of the chain, we can offer no opinion on that which we have had no opportunity of seeing. The question is after all of secondary importance since Hiuan-tsang takes us back to his starting point : "To the north-east of the city of Po-lu-sha 50 *li* or so, we come to a high mountain." Now to the north-east (or more exactly to the east-north-east, but we know our traveller was not so minutely accurate) rises the lofty peak of Karamār which attains a height of not less than 1030 metres, its very isolation together with the steepness of its southern slope increasing the grandeur of its appearance. One circumstance might make the unwarned reader hesitate. When calculating his distances, Hiuan-tsang very naturally took as his guiding mark the summit of the mountain : he put it as we have just seen "some fifty *li* or so" or a day's journey to the north-east just as a little before he fixed the summit of Tan-to-lo-kia at 20 *li* from Po-lu-sha in the same direction : now from the present village of Shāhbāz-gaṛhī to the summits of Mēkha-sanda and Karamār is, according to the map, 3 and 11 kilometres respectively, that is, at most nine and thirty-three *li*. The difference may appear somewhat great, but it must be remembered that Hiuan-tsang was not in the habit of travelling as the crow flies. He gained the summit of Mēkha-sanda only by climbing the rocky windings of the foot-path, and having spent a good hour, he very naturally calculated it as "20 *li*." As to Karamār, whoever has made the ascent will, as we did, deem the stage quite long enough and not dream of finding fault with Hiuan-tsang for his "fifty *li* or so."[2] Moreover it is well to bear in mind that when it was a question of estimating distances between given points, the good pilgrim, not possessing our maps, proceeded to guess or as we say, to estimate it. If one will but cast a glance at the profile which the hills in question present from Saval-Ḍhēr which is on the road just travelled by Hiuan-tsang the accuracy of his *coup d'œil* in this particular instance will be readily realized. Here again the topographical identification strengthening and in its turn supported by the sum of our previous arguments cannot be doubted.

By the help of the information given by Hiuan-tsang would it be possible to go further ? On "the mountain" he tells us, "is a figure of the wife of Iśvara Deva carved out of green (bluish) stone. This is Bhima Deva. All the people of the better class, and the lower orders too, declare that this figure was self wrought." It is impossible not to recognize, at once from this particular detail one of those *svayambhū* images (self-existing, *i.e.*, of natural formation) which, we have met in Kashmīr, where they are still so numerous and so venerated. On the road to

---

[1] *Loc. laud.*, p. 678.

[2] It is moreover a point noted over and over again by all who have had occasion to compare with our modern maps the necessarily approximate data of Hiuan-tsang that for him, as for all the old travellers, time was the principal basis for the estimating of distances. It might almost be stated as an axiom that his *li* is the shorter as the time taken to accomplish it is long, which is naturally the case among the mountains. M. Grenard remarks that Ptolemy working upon the itineraries of merchants "has extended the Pamīrs in an improbable way" (he estimates 24 degrees instead of 9) and that "in this same region the *li* of Hiuan-tsang is two or three times less than (what it is) in Kachgarie" where he travels on the plain (***Mission scientifique de la Haute-Asie***, II part, p. 17, n. 1.) - Cf. also Dr. Stein (*loc. laud.*, 37).

Amarnāth alone, for example, there are two of particular celebrity. One in the bed of the Liddar, is an enormous boulder which is supposed to represent Gaṇeśa. The other, a huge rock, situated more than 15,000 feet high, presenting vaguely the profile of a sitting man, passes for an image of Bhairava. The same must be understood of the eternally frozen springs, in the huge cave which is the aim of the pilgrimage : they are indeed, likewise believed to be self-created images of Śiva, his wife and his sons. Moreover when Hiuan-tsang adds to his account of this miraculous natural statue of Bhīmadevī that " a multitude of people come from every part of India to worship it " one would seem to be reading a description of the modern pilgrimage to Amarnāth where every year on the day of the full moon of Śrāvana (July-August) even now from all the corners of India, " people flock in crowds to pay their vows and seek prosperity thereby." There is still the same religious fervour, only its object has moved a hundred leagues to the east. But though Hiuan-tsang's account is most interesting for religious history, it is from the archæological point of view, most embarrassing. For in the absence of those marks and lines of red lead which the art of the officiating Brahmans ordinarily adds to nature, how is a *svayambhū* image to be distinguished from the most ordinary rock ? It would require the eye of faith which is not in one's power or the help of tradition, and this latter seems to be for ever lost among the Hindu *banya* population of the surrounding villages.

Nevertheless let us try and preferably examine the highest peak of the mountain. We find it surmounted by a cairn marking the trigonometrical survey station. Let us hope that the English engineers, in constructing it, have not inadvertently demolished the statue of Bhīmadevī. All round the summit exist the remains of walls ; immediately to the east is a *ziārat* surrounded by dry stone walls and decorated like a Tibetan shrine, with a profusion of little flags. It is still, it appears, much visited by the faithful, and the magnificent trees which still shade the summit of Karamār undoubtedly owe their preservation entirely to this sacred neighbour. On the south side fall rocky cliffs of vertiginous steepness all white with the droppings of huge vultures who delight to perch there. It would seem as if there was

Fig. 16. Summit of Karamār seen from Mēkha-sanda.

nothing to be found here. But what is it that the man accompanying us from Shiva has to relate concerning the miraculous leap that a *faqīr* once made from the top of these cliffs? This gives us a hint. Until recent years was it not the custom of many a *Sādhu* on his journey towards Amarnāth to make such a leap from the top of the *svayambhū* image of Bhairava into final deliverance? [1] We pursue our enquiries and the most serious minded people assure us that this feat was only one of many miracles performed by Yekeisāb the *pīr* of the hill, who, according to a particular inexplicable by Mahommedan ideas—and which seems a survival of the Śaivite legend—shares with his dog the reverence of the Pathāns of the neighbourhood.[2] In his youth his enemies by a ruse made him fall from the steep mountain-top and there he hung suspended from a bough above the abyss, death staring him in the face: one of his friends, "a female *faqīr*," gifted with supernatural power caught him unhurt at the foot of the hill in the skirt of her robe. Now the name of this guardian angel was no other than Sher-bānu, "the lady of the lion" that is to say exactly one of the common appellations of Bhimā the "redoubtable" yet benign goddess.[3]

In these extravagant stories we cannot but catch glimpses of confused and distorted extracts from the *māhātmya* [4] of Bhimadevī, certainly not as Hiuan-tsang must have known it, but as those forcibly converted by the first Mahommedan invaders had modified it in their desire to reconcile their new religion with their traditional customs. It seems as if we have in this Yekeisāb one of those semi-Mahommedan semi-Hindu saints, half *sādhu*, half *faqīr* whose legends are most frequently grafted on an Indian stock and who are so numerous all over north-western India. Without going further afield, we have a *pīr* of not less doubtful character in that Shāhbāz-Kalendar whom Bāber, though himself not very orthodox, accuses of having perverted the not yet stable faith of a number of Yūsufzais and Dilazāks: accordingly in 1519 on the occasion of his first visit he considered it his duty to destroy the tomb of this heretic.[5] As to Yekeisāb, if we are to believe the grey beards of the villages, he lived "seven hundred years ago in the time of Timur." As the invasion of India by this latter dates from 1398 we have to choose. But we should only bear in mind that the saint of Karamâr would thus date back to that indecisive period which extends from the destruction of the Hindu Kingdom of Kābul and Peshawar by Mahmud of Ghazni in the 11th Century to the final settlement of the Pathān tribes in this district in the 15th Century. In this interval the legend which undoubtedly had remained deep rooted until the downfall of the Śāhi kings—one of whom bore the name of Bhīmadeva—had had time to disguise itself as Mussalman. When the Pathāns had completely made the Peshawar District as well as the remainder of Afghanistan, a stronghold of pure Sunni belief it is not

---

[1] There are "leaps of Bhairava" in several parts of India, at Girnar for instance, *Indian Antiquary*, 1901, p. 241.

[2] It is known that Siva and his spouse delight in sometimes taking terrible forms and again the appearance of people belonging to the most despised castes or even outcasts and for whom contact with dogs is no defilement: one of the legends of Kashmir will have it that the divine couple have been met with on the heights disguised as Chamars and engaged in milking a bitch.

[3] Cf. the names *siṃhayānā, siṃhavahinī*, etc., given to Pārvatī, Uma, Gaurī, Durgā, Bhīmā, etc., or whatever name by which one may wish to designate the wife of Śiva, who is always accompanied by a lion which usually serves as her vehicle.

[4] As is known the term *māhātmya* is applied to a species of guide or handbook generally written in Sanskrit which describes the sites of *tīrthas* or places of pilgrimage in India explaining the sacred legends connected with them and at the same time exalting their merits and virtues.

[5] See his *Memoirs* translation, Erskine, p. 252 or translation, Pavet de Courteille, Vol. I. p. 284. The tom of Shāhbāz rose above the hill which bears the inscription of Aśoka near Shāhbāz-Gaṛhī.

surprising that under the guise of a *pīr* there should have survived the local remembrance of the "lady of the lion." On the other hand it is not less probable that the *ziārat* of Yekeisāb and his dog has actually appropriated on the summit of the hill, the traditional celebrity and miraculous powers, if not the actual spot, of the temple of Bhīma-devī. If we were in Kashmīr where Mussalman shrines never fail to mark ancient Hindu sites we should say we were quite sure.[1]

But now where was the temple of Śiva or Maheśvara which our traveller meets "below the mountain" sacred to the cult of his wife. On such a vague indication we do not pretend to be able to fix its site. Let us note however that the summit of Karamār is accessible from only two sides. On the north a spur stops all access, while the southern slope is only practicable for goats and their shepherds. Only a footpath still crosses by its greatest width from west to east the long ridge of the mountain. Coming from Po-lu-sha on his way to Udabhāṇḍa, it was by this road that Hiuan-tsang must inevitably, have ascended and descended. Now, if travelling in the same direction as he, we allow ourselves to be brought back to the plain by this single road from the summit of Karamār, the first village we reach "below the mountain" bears precisely the name of Shiva (English map Shewa). Undoubtedly to the minds of the present day Mussalmans this word represents nothing but the leguminous tree commonly called (*shisham*, *Dalbergia Sissou*, Roxb.). Does there not lie hidden under cover of this double meaning some remembrance of the name of Śiva? We should not be prepared to swear to it.[2]

Be that as it may, it is from the sanctuary of Bhīmā and not from that of Maheśvara, that is from the summit and not from the foot of the mountain, that Hiuan-tsang now calculates in a south-easterly direction a hundred and fifty *li* (*viz.*, thirty miles or fifty kilometres—that is three stages) to Udabhāṇḍa. Consequently it took the same time to reach there from the top of Bhīmadevīparvata as from Po-lu-sha, which, according to Song-yun, was three days travel west of the Indus.[3] As the summit of the hill was itself a day's journey from Po-lu-sha, it comes finally to this that from Po-lu-sha to Udabhāṇḍa four stages had to be reckoned if, *en route* the ascent of the Bhīmadevīparvata was made, while only three if one travelled by the plain. One need not be a professional alpinist to understand this. But the question still remains: how could three stages or one hundred and fifty *li* be found between Shāhbāz-gaṛhī and Und?

Certainly it cannot be denied that if, as Beal[4] wishes, thirty miles are "projected" to the north-west of Und, it brings us eight miles further than Po-lu-sha as far as the well known ruins which overlook Jamāl-gaṛhī. Why should not this hill be the Bhīmadevīparvata? Eight miles more to the south-west the not less famous ruins of Takht-i-Bāhī would, in their turn, represent Po-lu-sha. It is true

---

[1] This is, however, not peculiar to Kashmir and applies more or less to the whole of the Punjab and to that part of Central Asia which had embraced Islam only after having been indianized. M. Grenard (*loc. laud.*, III part, p. 844) remarks *à propos* of Kachgarie there can hardly have been a Buddhist temple, monastery or hermitage of any note where there is not to-day a mosque or a mazār. Dr. Stein likewise writes, "The tenacity of local worship has proved in Khotan quite as helpful for my enquiries into questions of ancient topography as it has in Kashmi." (*J. R. A. S.*, 1901, p. 296).

[2] It must be remembered that the Sanskrit Ś is a surd fricative (like the Z in azure) and consequently closely akin to Ṣ or sh.

[3] Translation, Beal I, p. CII. "Thirteen" is a slip for "three."

[4] *Loc. laud.*, I. p. 114, n 108.

that we should not then be able to make anything of Tan-to-lo-kia nor of Pushkarāvatī nor in consequence of Purushapura : but never mind : it would really be too ungracious to admit that Hiuan-tsang does not say a word about the two greatest discoveries made in this region during the last fifty years. Nevertheless we must reconcile ourselves to it and also bear in mind that our traveller did not "project" himself through space in the manner of the ancient *arhats*, by aerial paths. He very prosaically followed the road : now that the road takes nearly thirty miles or fifty kilometres between Shāhbāz-gaṛhī and Und, we have, like him, some reason to believe, as we have travelled it.[1] The reason is that it takes the longest way : very wisely it avoids leading the confiding traveller across that wilderness of stony dunes known locally as the "*Mairah*" but winding leisurely along it follows the succession of wells or skirts the banks of the rivers. The journey gains in comfort what it loses in directness. What harm if the journey be a third longer if the fatigue be only half ? And if it does take a day longer, what does it matter ? Besides, everyone knows that in the East time is of no consequence.

This old route from Und to Shāhbāz-garhī is still a very tangible reality[2] but even if it no longer existed, grounds would not be lacking for imagining its existence. A decisive proof of the long circuit it described towards the east in order to reach Und from the north would be further supplied us, by what Hiuan-tsang tells us of Śalātura. He places the birthplace of Pāṇini, twenty *li* to the north-west of Udabhāṇḍa on the very spot where now stands the large village of Lahor about seven kilometres from Und. The present village is conspicuous from afar by reason of a huge *ḍhērī* which we found in regular exploitation like all of its kind in the north-west ; and if the derivation of the name is not entirely satisfactory, there is no doubt as to the antiquity of the site and its identification.[3] But the point we wish to emphasise is that, in order to go from Udabhāṇḍa to Śalātura, Hiuan-tsang had to make a special excursion. Consequently he did not meet this spot on his route when coming from Po-lu-sha. Now Lahor is exactly to the north-west of Und, that is precisely in the direction of Shāhbāz-gaṛhī and the pilgrim must have passed it, had he come in a straight line. But he was far too experienced a traveller not to know that the straight line is hardly ever the best road from one point to another and, like everyone else, he took the longest way.

Thus forewarned, nothing is simpler for us than to follow on the map the sequence of his journey. The first day he must have been content with descending from the top of the Bhīmadevīparvata and regaining by way of Shiva the same stage, as if he had set out that morning from Po-lu-sha. The second stage led him most probably to the neighbourhood of Swābi which is still the traditional ḥalting place : the third day by way of the valley of the Bhadrai, he reached the bank of the Indus. On the right bank of the river rose a rich and busy town which Hiuan-

[1] It was only by slightly forcing the marches that we were able to reach Hoti-Mardan from Und in three stages. The former eight kilometres to the west of Shāhbāz-gaṛhī is the new head-quarters of the English administration.

[2] See the accompanying map, and for a photograph of the road, *Sur la frontière indo-afghane*, Fig. 7.

[3] Analogy with the name of the capital of the Punjab "the big Lahore" as it is called in the district must have influenced the change from Salātura to Lahore. Let us here remark that had not the name of Panini's birthplace been known from another source Stan. Julien could never have recognized the correct transcription Śalātura under Hiuan-tsang's P'o-lo-tu-lo which must be corrected to So-lo-tu-lo. For a view of the present Afghan village see *Sur la frontière indo-afghane*, Fig. 5.

tsang, in his but little flexible language calls Ou-to-kia-han-t'cha and in which Dr. Stein has rightly recognized the Udabhāṇḍapura to which the *Rājataraṅgiṇi* refers as the winter capital of the Śāhī kings of Kabul.[1] Only the Chinese transcription suggests an optional form Udakabhāṇḍa. The text seems even to make an allusion to the name of the town which would be expressed in old French by "*marchandise de l'eau.*" Here is found, we read "a supply of valuable wares and the different nations of India bring in quantities their rarest and most esteemed products." Moreover, one cannot fail to recognize in the Und of to-day, for thus it is called by its present inhabitants—the more refined people of Peshawar and Mardān pronounce it Ohind—the Wayhand of Alberūni, the Udabhāṇḍa of the Kashmīr chronicle, and the Udakabhāṇḍa of the Chinese pilgrim. The ancient village is not without traces of its former splendour from the time when it was one of the great markets of Indian trade with Central Asia. It is true that the circumvallation of dry stone walls is not more than twelve hundred metres, very far indeed from the twenty *li* circumference allotted to the ancient town by Hiuan-tsang. But in the high banks of the Indus portions of walls of Græco-Buddhist construction break through everywhere:[2] in the sands of the river bank coins of the Indo-Greeks and Indo-Scythians are freely found along with those of the Hindu kings of Kashmīr and of Kābul; a permanent ferry still crosses the huge bed broken by sandbanks, where the Sindhu extends for more than three kilometres, although its waters are occasionally fordable during the winter season;[3] and the remembrance is still preserved of the significant name which the first Mussalman invaders gave to the now decayed city: the gate of India, *Dvār-i-Hind.*

Conclusion.

Now we have come to the limit of Gandhāra. The river passed, we are in reality in the plain of Chach the ancient country of Chuksha and in the territory of Takshaśilā which is reached in three stages.[4] We will therefore leave our fellow

[1] See *Fest-gruss* an R. von Routh, p. 199. The transcription given by Hiuan-tsang aud which Stan. Julien has proposed to read Udakhāṇḍa, is not, iu reality, so far removed from the form given by the Rājataraṅgiṇī as might be believed. At first sight the Chinese characters seem to exclude the restoration of a labial but it is not so. M. Ed. Chavannes has observed that we possess in a country adjacent to Gandhāra an analogous case. The country which Hiuan-tsang denominates Kie-p'an-t'o is sometimes called simply Han-t'o (cf. the *T'ong-tien* of Tou-Yeou mentioned in the *Pien-i-tien*, chap. LXVII, pl. V.); now, in this case the same character *han* which, we see appear in Ou-to-kia-han-t'cha corresponds to the *p'an* of the fuller form, that is a labial. Hiuan-tsang's transcription exactly coincides with an original Sanskrit Udakabbhāṇḍa. As for the use of *uda*° instead of *udaka*° at the beginning of a compound it is much too ordinary for the co-existence of two optional forms Udakabhāṇḍa aud Udabhāṇḍa to surprise us. These observations completely sweep away every vestige of foundation for the hypothesis of Colonel Deane who, setting aside the opiniou held by Reinaud, Vivien de Saint Martin, Cunningham and Dr. Stein endeavours to find iu the village of Khunda, "about six miles north-west (?) from Hund" a remembrance of the imaginary form Udakhāṇḍa (*loc. laud.*, p. 673).

[2] For a specimen see *Sur la frontière indo-afghane* Fig. 4.

[3] Hiuan-tsang on his returu journey crossed the Iudus on an elephant an animal commonly used in India for the crossing of fords (see *Biographie* translation, Stan. Julien, p. 263). Bāber on the occasion of his first invasion in the same way forded the stream with his camels and horses: but this took place in February: during the floods of summer it would be impossible. As for the ferry cf. Bellew, *loc. laud.*, p. 16; Abbott, *J. B. A. S.* 1854, p. 337, etc. Let us mention incidentally that the width given by Hiuan-tsang to the Indus, *viz.*, "three or four *li*" [translation Stan. Julien II, p. 151, the biographer gives "four or five *li*" (*ibid* I, p. 263) and Stan. Julien believed he ought to apologise for the exaggeration !] is, at the present time, much less than the reality. Most travellers seeing the Indus at Attock only, where it attains a width of less than three huudred metres can have no idea that a few leagues up stream it is ten times wider and correspondingly shallower.

Concerning the identification, due to Dr. Stein, of Cac or, according to common orthography, Chach (pronounced Tchatch) with Chuksha see *Indian Antiquary* 1896, p. 174. Takshaśila has long ago been identified by Cunningham with Shāh ḍhērī, near Kāla-ka-Serai station on the North Western Railway (*A. S. I.* II, p. III, *Anc. Geog. of India*, p. III). It would have been equally interesting to follow Hiuan-tsang on the road which to the north of Und led him, across the moun-

traveller at the moment when he arrives at the threshold of the promised land : an this will not be without regret. We were getting accustomed to his tastes and habits of travel, to his craving for edification, his foible for monkish stories, his complete disdain of ruins and his very obvious preference for beaten tracks and stages of reasonable length. Perhaps also we were becoming familiar with the methods he uses in editing his itinerary. If his calculations are necessarily approximate, if many of his indications are, it must be confessed, somewhat vague, there is not one which, tested on the spot itself, does not prove perfectly truthful and sufficiently exact. Thus, thanks to the precision and the honesty of his journal we have been able to follow him from beginning to end in his travel through Gandhāra, availing ourselves at each step of the information which he has recorded and the legends which he has collected, in order to determine the principal trade routes and identify the most celebrated among the Buddhist monuments of the country. The sanctuaries of Kanishka, of the "Eye-gift," of Hāritī, of Viśvantara, etc., place themselves as it were, on the map for the use of archæologists, awaiting methodical excavation, of which the era seems at last to dawn. For the historian it is not less interesting to trace the modern changes of the high-roads. It is but yesterday that the new road to Swāt, Dīr and Chitrāl, which as far as Dargai a narrow gauge railway has just doubled, has begun to supplant its ancient rivals on the right and left, and that Nowshera and Hoti Mardān have taken the place of Pushkarāvatī and Po-lu-sha. It is from a period as recent as that of Akbar that the facilities offered by the narrow gorge at Attock for a permanent bridge, either a bridge of boats or of iron, attracted the attention of the Mughals, even before that of the English, and definitely diverted the main commercial route between Central Asia and India towards this place to the ultimate ruin of Und. But, as we have already had occasion to remark, there is nothing more artificial than the alignment of the Grand Trunk Road and of the railway, mostly bridges and embankments straight across marshes and ravines, a triumph indeed of the straight line and a feat of engineering skill. But the old route, the natural way, that of the fords of winter and the ferries of summer, described a great curve to the north, across the gently undulating plain which saw flow by the tide of so many invasions. By no means the least service rendered by Hiuan-tsang to a correct understanding of the ancient geography of India has been that of fixing clearly for his time, from the Khyber Pass to the Indus, the four main stages : Purushapura, Pushkarāvatī, Po-lu-sha and Udabhāṇḍa.

---

tains and the Bunēr Valley, to the capital of Udyāna. But we have been able to visit only a corner of the recently opened Swāt valley and we must refer to the notes of Colonel Deane and Dr. Stein the only archæologists who have penetrated into Upper Swāt and Bunēr on the occasion of the last English expeditions. We show specially on our map the identifications proposed by Dr. Stein for the three great sanctuaries which Hiuan-tsang mentions in Bunēr. At the risk of correction we add to them a fourth which, in our opinion, fixes itself, namely mount Hi-lo with mount Ilam. In the translations by S. Julien and Beal, Hiuan-tsang mentions with reference to Maṅgalapura, in going southwards first mount Hi-lo at four hundred *li* then the Mahāvana *saṅghārāma* at two hundred *li*. We think it should be read in increasing progression that the first is at one hundred *li* and the second at two hundred *li*. This reading agrees entirely with Hiuan-tsang's methods of editing the journal, with the name of Ilam and its distance with reference to Manglaor and with the progress of the itinerary of the pilgrim who setting out from the Mahāvana carries us no longer towards the south but leads us steadily to the north-west towards the valley of Chan-n-ilo-che (now Adinzai) in the Swāt country.

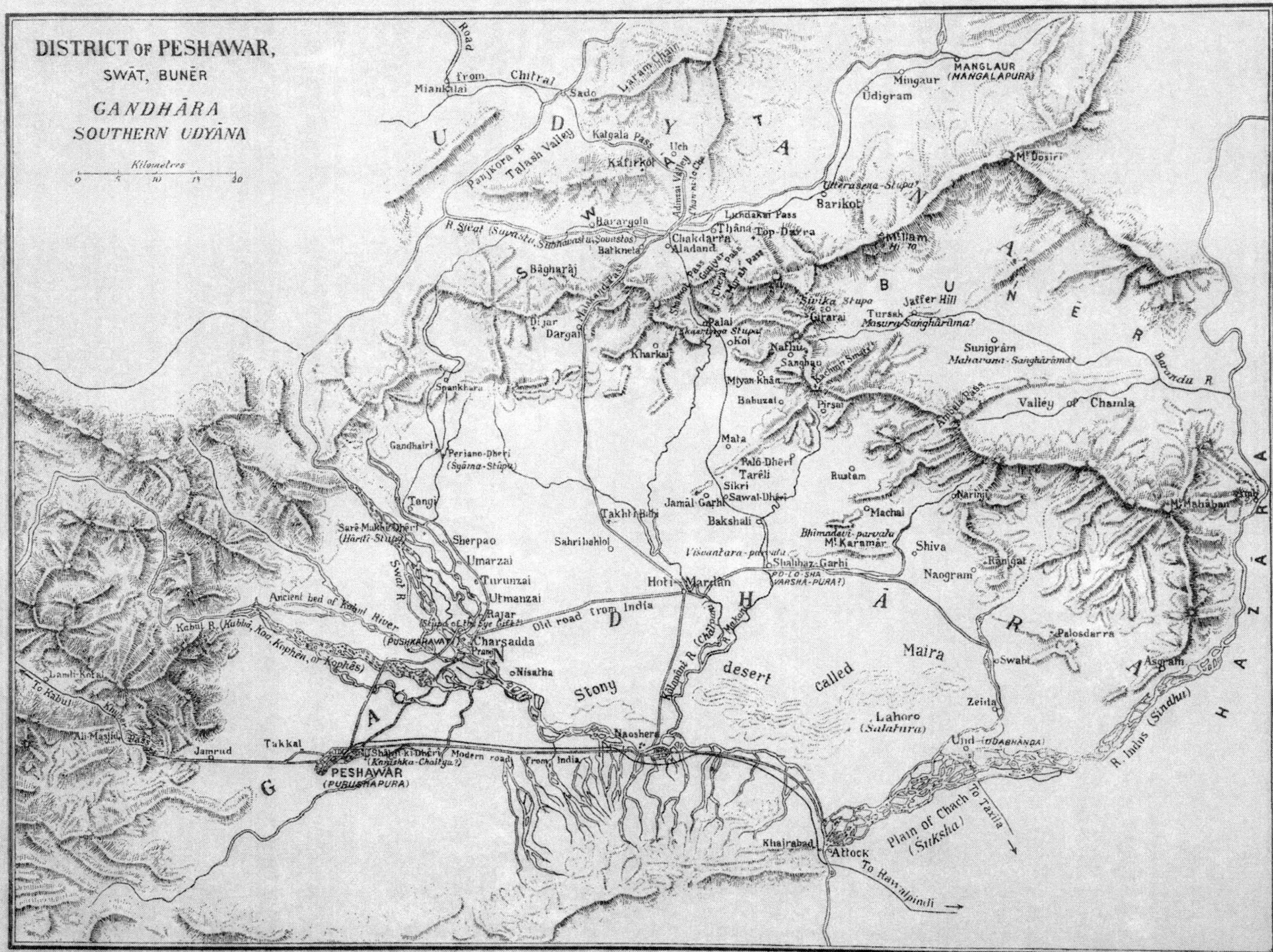
DISTRICT OF PESHAWAR,
SWĀT, BUNĒR
GANDHĀRA
SOUTHERN UDYĀNA
Kilometres
0 5 10 15 20
UDYĀNA
SWĀT
BUNĒR
GANDHĀRA
HAZĀRA
Road from Chitral
Miankalai
Sado
Laram Chain
Panjkora R.
Talash Valley
Katgala Pass
Uch
Katirkot
Adinzai Valley
Barargola
R. Swāt (Suvastu, Subhavastu, Soastos)
Chakdarra
Aladand
Thāna
Top-Darra
Lundakai Pass
Barikot
Uttarasena-Stupa?
Udigram
Mingaur
MANGLAUR (MANGALAPURA)
Mt Dosiri
Mt Ilam
Bagharaj
Malakand Pass
Dargai
Palai
Koi
Kharkai
Girarai
Sirika Stupa
Tursak
Masura Sangharama?
Jaffer Hill
Sunigram
Maharana-Sangharama?
Barandu R.
Valley of Chamla
Ambela Pass
Nathu
Sanghao
Miyan-Khān
Babuzai
Pirsai
Mala
Palō-Dhērī
Tarēli
Sikri
Sawal-Dhēri
Jamal Garhi
Bakshali
Takht-i-Bahi
Sahri-bahlol
Rustam
Narinji
Machai
Bhimadevi-parvata
Mt Karamar
Shiva
Rāngai
Naogram
Mt Mahaban
Visvantara-parvata
Shahbaz-Garhi
PO-LO-SHA (VARSHA-PURA?)
Hoti-Mardan
Palosdarra
Swabi
Asgram
Zeida
Und (UDABHANDA)
Lahoro (Salatura)
Stony desert called Maira
R. Indus (Sindhu)
Plain of Chach (Suksha)
To Taxila
Attock
Khairabad
To Rawalpindi
Naoshera
Kalapani R. (Chalpani)
Old road from India
Modern road from India
Gandhairi
Periano-Dhēri (Syama-Stupa)
Spankhara
Tangi
Sarē-Makhi-Dhēri (Hariti-Stupa)
Sherpao
Umarzai
Turunzai
Utmanzai
Rajar
Swāt R.
Stupa of the Eye Gift
(PUSHKARAVATI)
Charsadda
Nisatha
Ancient bed of Kabul River
Kabul R. (Kubha, Koa, Kophēn, or Kophēs)
Landi-Kotal
To Kabul
Khaibar Pass
Ali-Masjid
Jamrud
Takkal
Shāh-ji-ki-Dhēri (Kanishka-Chaitya?)
PESHAWAR (PURUSHAPURA)